zen

and the art of
travel

zen

and the art of

travel

eric chaline

SOURCEBOOKS, INC.
NAPERVILLE, ILLINOIS

contents

Introduction

"He who would bring
home the wealth
of the Indies,

must carry the wealth of
the Indies with him."

Simon Brown

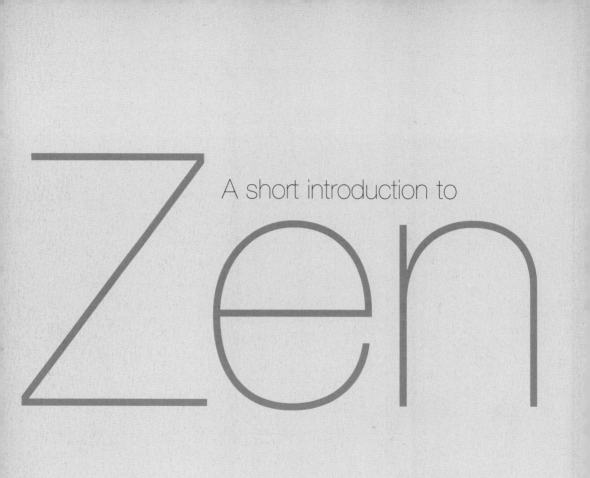

A short introduction to Zen

Zen Buddhism started around about the fifth century A.D. in China and is based on the practice of sudden enlightenment, known as satori, which is achieved through meditation. It holds that the consciousness is "real" (objects are not) and that the mind should have no pre-formed thoughts or feelings but, rather, the Zen practitioner should be receptive through meditation without comment. Thus Zen is a way of experiencing rather than a doctrine of ideas based on experience. A traditional way for students to understand Zen teachings was through a koan—a subject for meditation, often appearing in the form of a paradoxical saying. Students were then encouraged to meditate on this saying to help them to find enlightenment.

Zen

From John Bunyan's *Pilgrim's Progress* to the ancient Chinese Dao, the Way, the physical act of travel has been used as a metaphor for humanity's spiritual quest for enlightenment. The two activities have many similarities. Both the pilgrim and the traveler set off into the unknown, leaving behind the familiar world of family and friends. They encounter setbacks on the road, make new acquaintances who either help or hinder them, discover new and unexpected worlds, and finally arrive at their respective "promised lands." In the act of pilgrimage, the physical and spiritual journeys are combined. Zen, however, is a state of mind unrelated to the physical. It is the act of journeying that takes us toward enlightenment.

and the art of travel

In bringing together travel and Zen, this book seeks to illuminate both how the Zen mind can transform our experience of travel and, equally, how travel can bring us to a better understanding of Zen. The travelers' tales contained in this book are experiences to be considered, in a similar way to the koan, and are as captivating as they are illuminating so that you will be able to enjoy a good "yarn" on your road to enlightenment. The vignettes themselves are not wholly practical, but each chapter closes with useful advice for the traveler on subjects such as packing and eating, as well as traveling by train or bus over several continents.

"A famous scholar came to learn about Zen. The teacher served him tea. He filled the cup with tea, and carried on pouring so that the cup overflowed. 'It is full! No more will go in!' the scholar said.'Like this cup,' the teacher said, 'you are full of your own opinions. How can I teach you about Zen unless you first empty your cup?'"

Simon Brown

chapter 1

right thought: preparation

meditation: "A great tailor cuts little." Tao te Ching

Zen is itself a journey that takes us along unknown paths, through unfamiliar lands, to meetings with strangers, to yet stranger destinations. On this voyage of self-discovery nothing is guaranteed, least of all that we shall reach the place upon which we have set our sights. In the very act of wanting to arrive, we may stumble or lose our way, or we may lose heart and abandon the road in despair. Travelers in the physical world are far more fortunate: equipped with passports, money, and tickets, they are almost certain of arriving at their destinations. But how should they be outfitted for their journey? What should they take with them, and more importantly, what should they leave behind?

"Don't rely on others
to show you the way,

carry your own map."

David Baird

rites of passage

At the age of sixteen, I boldly announced that I would be going away on my own. The son of divorced parents, I was supposed to spend one month of the summer vacation with my father and one with my mother and stepfather, who had just bought a flat in Antibes on the French Riviera. I felt too old for yet another family holiday, and I longed for an adventure that would cut the maternal apron strings and mark my entry into adulthood. I arrived in France in a sulk. In the 1970s, the south of France was a popular destination during the summer months. From June through September, the string of coastal resorts on the Cote d'Azure—Nice, Antibes, Juan-les-Pins, Cannes, and Saint-Tropez—were crowded, but not in an interesting way.

Antibes was no longer the society playground it had been in 1925 when F. Scott Fitzgerald had joked, "There is no one at Antibes this summer except me, Zelda, the Valentinos, the Murphys, Mistinguette, Rex Ingram, Dos Passos, Alice Terry, The MacLeishes, Charlie Brackett, Maud Kahn, Esther Murphy, Marguerite Namara, E. Philips Oppenheim, Mannes the violinist, Floyd Dell, Max and Crystal Eastman, ex-premier Orlando, Etienne de Beaumont—just a real place to rough it and escape from the world."

The British and American artists, movie stars, and socialites had all departed long before. Their elegant villas on the Cap d'Antibes, tucked behind their high permieter walls and hedges, had been sold to Arab princes at inflated prices, and the sea-front promenades were thronged by French, Scandinavian, and German families, drawn in by fair attractions, games arcades, and fast food outlets.

Already bored of the daily routine of beach followed by an after-dinner stroll on the sea-front, I was thumbing through the books in the local bookshop when I came across a series of books entitled *Topo-guides des sentiers de grandes randonnée*. The neat, slim numbered volumes gave detailed instructions on how to walk from the French Riviera to the Pas de Calais—a journey of 625 miles through the heartlands of France—and a promise from the publishers, the French Hiking Federation, that you would never have to enter a town nor set foot on as asphalted road (although they added you would never be more than twelve miles from civilization).

My imagination had been set ablaze. I was there, on the road, alongside the English poet laureate John Masefield (1878–1967) who, when on his way to the market town of Tewkesbury had exulted:

"It is good to be out on the road,
and going one knows not where,
Going through meadow and village,
One knows not whither nor why."

horizon

In 1846 Charles Dickens described Aix-en-Provence, in France, as "…very clean; but so hot and so intensely light, that when I walked out at noon it was like suddenly coming from the darkened room into crisp blue fire. The air was so very clear that distant hills and rocky points appeared within an hour's walk; while the town immediately at hand—with a kind of blue wind between me and it—seemed to be white hot, and to be throwing off a fiery air from the surface."

As I sat in a narrow pool of shade on the slopes of the Mount St Victoire, I let my surroundings inspire my imagination. I wondered what it must have been like for monks who had to bring up all their supplies on foot from the valley to the hilltop monastery that had stood here for centuries. I gulped in the view of Aix-en-Provence and the plain beyond, which seemed all the better because I had climbed for three hours to earn it. The cicadas entertained me with their rasping choruses, and tiny green lizards scampered around my feet, darting to snatch crumbs from my meal. This is it! I thought to myself, and I knew there and then that I was hooked. I had become one of those people who, to use the analogy penned by the formidable traveler and author Freya Starke, looked at the horizon and saw not an insurmountable obstacle but something to go beyond.

inspiration

Mountains have always inspired those with a religious inclination.

For
t h e
literally
minded   they
seem   physically
closer to heaven and to
the gods, and to the mystic
their size and timelessness
speaks of something infinitely
greater than man. I, like countless
others before me, had been touched by
that sense of climbing a mountain to find a
"higher truth." Mount Sainte-Victoire, in France,
attracted one of its most famous sons, the painter Paul
Cézanne, to return to it time and time again though, in his
case, it was in search of artistic rather than religious salvation.
Years later in an art gallery in New York, I read a description of
Cézanne, by Meyer Schapiro: "[He] identified with it as the ancients with
a holy mountain on which they set the dwelling or birthplace of a god. Only
for Cézanne it was an inner god that he externalized in this mountain peak—his
striving and exaltation and desire for repose." In his own mind, Cézanne never fully
attained his goal. He never found his salvation on Mount Sainte-Victoire, leaving most of
his works unfinished and destroying many others.

"Amid the mountains of high summer,

I bowed respectfully before

The tall clogs of a statue,

Asking a blessing on my journey."

Matsuo Basho

Reaching
for the
Stars

★ ★ ★ ★ ★

Unusually for the time of year in France, the weather began to take a turn for the worse; the skies darkened as great piles of gray rain clouds were blown in by the Mistral wind. I awoke one morning to find that it was pouring with rain. I decided to leave the path I was hiking and head for the nearest highway, where I thumbed a ride. Within a couple of hours and two or three lifts, I had reached Avignon, the ancient seats of popes and schismatic anti popes between the fourteenth and fifteenth centuries. After looking at the bridge that half-spans the Rhone, made famous by the child's playground song, "Sur le pont d'Avignon, on-y danse, on y danse…," I went to the great rambling Palais des Papes, a building that has failed to impress a succession of foreign visitors: in 1822, Henry James found it "as desolate as it was dirty," and in 1926, Arnold Bennett, "unpleasant, mean, and particularly medieval."

It was festival time in Avignon. The city was full of people and performance artists; every square and plaza had been transformed into a makeshift amphitheater for a concert or a play. Staying in a city was, however, much more expensive than hiking through the countryside, and within a few days, I was running dangerously low on money. My journey had come to an abrupt end and, rather than return to my parents whom I had boldly left two weeks before, I hitchhiked to Paris and spent the last of my money buying a ticket for the night train back to London. I had reached my goal—freedom—but this journey had taught me more.

alone

I realized that I was the only one truly responsible for my fate on earth If I made a mistake and got lost or became injured, ran out of food or money or, conversely, had a great time, then there was no one to blame or praise but myself. Until then, I had not even been aware that I habitually left decisions affecting my life to other people—my parents and teachers. I realized that many adults relinquish power over their lives to others, such as their spouse or employer.

"If you will be a traveller,
    have always
        the eyes of a falcon,
        the ears of an ass,
        the face of an ape,
        the mouth of a hog,
        the shoulder of a camel,
        the legs of a stag
            and see that you never want
            two bags very full,
                that is one of patience
                and another of money."

John Florio (1591)

rituals

"Hello," came an unmistakably British voice. "Are you English? Do come up." The solid house lay in an isolated Provence hamlet so small that it had neither a shop nor a paved road. I discovered it had been rented for the summer by a party of four English schoolteachers. "We'll be having tea when my friends get back. Would you like to join us?" she asked. This was not merely the offer of a cup of tea, but an invitation to join them for an important social occasion. The three other residents introduced themselves, and tea was prepared in the English fashion.

Just as the *chanoyu*, the tea ceremony, epitomizes Japanese culture, so afternoon tea is an English ritual. The *chanoyu* begins with the display of the tea implements and teabowls. My English hosts had brought everything from home: dark-brown India tea, a kettle and teapot, and, of course, their own mugs. We discussed the gas stove, which was their only source of power, and the well water which they thought unsuitable for a proper "cuppa," although it was probably a great deal purer than at home.

Every culture has its rituals, great and small. I had seen family and friends prepare tea thousands of times without giving the act a second thought. It had taken a journey of many hundreds of miles to France to make me realize that teatime was the ritual that best defined the English.

It may be agreeable for
certain people to live a
retired life in a quiet place
away from noise and
disturbance. But it is certainly more

praiseworthy and courageous to practice Buddhism
living among your fellow
beings, helping them and
being of service to them.

Walpola Sri Rahula

leaving
fear behind

On my first trip as a teenager I was away for about two weeks but thought that I had been on a two-month adventure. In my short time as a lone wanderer, I had been the beneficiary of many acts of random kindness from total strangers including a couple who invited me to squeeze into their tiny tent on a rainy night and many free meals and drinks given to me by other travelers as well as local inhabitants. I had taken little with me outside of a change of clothes and a book. More important than what I had taken with me was what I left behind: my fear of the unknown—the fear that I could not make it and the fear of strangers—that every middle-class child learns from an early age. I then learned that the traveler, while not taking unnecessary risks, must unlearn these fears to set their minds free.

" A traveller without observation...

... is a bird without wings."

Saad

Fitting into the

Landscape

For many tens of thousands of years, our ancestors were nomads wandering over the face of the earth, following the great migrating herds of animals that they hunted. Walking, and not sitting at desks, is what humans are designed to do best. In plunging oneself completely into the environment, walking is the most immediate and engrossing form of travel. Since my first walking trip, I have hiked on four continents, over every sort of terrain, and in every sort of weather. Needless to say, my packing skills and the quality of the equipment I take with me have improved considerably with age and experience (and an increase in resources). The pleasure I get from walking is the same each time: the sense of fitting into the landscape—whether it be city of country—rather than passing fleetingly through it in a car or a train. I feel as if I belong there and am not just a "tourist."

Traveling

To close this first meditation on planning
and preparation for a journey, I will quote
the salutory warning given by another British
traveler, Lawrence Durrell:

"Journeys, like artists, are born and not made. A
thousand differing circumstances contribute to
them, few of them willed or determined by the
will—whatever we may think."

practicals: Guidebooks

Popular titles include "in-the-know" guides published by Lonely Planet, Let's Go, and the Rough Guide, which provide practical advice and information on the most remote destinations. Supplement your guide book with other sources— fellow travelers, or a helpful resident. A good person to start with is your hotel receptionist who, apart from speaking English, is likely to make sense of your request for an "inexpensive, typical restaurant," and not send you to the local branch of MacDonald's.

Buy a guidebook bearing in mind: size and weight, durability of binding, detail and

legibility of maps, and clarity of information on transport, currency, climate, security, and major attractions. On my own travels, my guides have sometimes been travel writers but more usually historians. These let me transpose historical information over the area that I'm visiting.

A final note of caution that is applicable for most of the Near East, Central Asia and India: beware men offering unsolicited directions and assistance: they come bearing carpets.

practicals: Packing

If your destination is the Near East, Central Asia, or the sub-continent, and your traveling style falls between backpacking and air-conditioned luxury, you might find the following packing guidelines useful. Make do with a single piece of luggage that will fit in a plane's overhead locker. This saves time, effort, and the hassle of lost luggage, allowing you to change and freshen up before arriving. Get the best your money can buy. I have traveled with two types: mountaineering backpacks suited for holidays that involve a lot of moving from place to place, and the flight attendant's case with wheels and an extendible handle for more sedentary trips. Include a small day pack for excursions, and a "fanny bag," of good-quality breathable material with an internal waterproof lining (for reasons of security—it should be large enough to hold passport, wallet, and other important documents).

Although you may be happiest spending most of your time in shorts, remember that there will be occasions when you will be expected to cover legs, arms, and head, such as when traveling through Islamic countries.

- two pairs of shorts
- pair of lightweight pants or long skirt
- long-sleeve shirt or blouse
- headgear
- walking boots
- beachwear
- fleece
- waterproof jacket
- T-shirts, socks, and underwear
- toilet bag and medical kit
- army knife
- hand-towel
- small backpack

chapter 2

right action: journeys

meditation: "The mind is everything, what you think, you become." Buddha

When our lives are running on automatic, following the cozy routine of workaday weeks and homebody weekends, the pattern of our perceptions also falls into well-worn grooves. We neatly segment time and apportion it to our daily activities. Space collapses into the microcosm of the commute, the neighborhood, or maybe the mall. Our personal geography relegates the immensity of the planet to tiny ink dots on the far horizon, while we keep the familiar in the foreground. Although the brain receives a constant stream of information about the world from the senses, it detaches itself from the flow of space-time. It then freeze-frames the moment, creating a "state"—a permanent "I" who could be, for example, "a successful manager," a "happily married mother of three," or an "unemployable failure." But in travel, the world seems to expand and maybe, just maybe, so do we.

"The difference between

landscape and landscape is small,

but there is a great difference

between the beholders."

Ralph Waldo Emerson

time travel

To borrow Paul Theroux's analogy of an airplane flight, we have all become "time travelers."

He adds wryly that little need or can be said about flying. "Anything remarkable would be disastrous, so you define a good flight by negatives. You didn't crash, you didn't get hijacked, you didn't throw up, you weren't late, and you weren't nauseated by the food." Modern travelers have a degree of comfort and convenience undreamed of by their forebears and they only have a small physical price to pay—a few days of jet lag. But what they have traded for all this extra time, comfort, and safety is the opportunity to experience the gradual detachment from their everyday lives and surroundings.

As a child of the late-twentieth century, most of the journeys that I have made have been of the "time-travel" variety, with little chance to collect my thoughts before it is time to de-plane at my destination. Nevertheless, I have on occasion been able to opt for more ancient and leisurely forms of travel in which the journey itself, while it may have a geographic beginning and ending, is its own end.

"A student asked his teacher,

'All the Buddhas enter the

one road of enlightenment.

Where does that road begin?'

'Here it is!' the teacher said,

drawing the figure one in the

air with his stick."

Zen saying

soul of the

On the three-day train journeys from London to the south of Spain that I took with my mother as a youngster, the world of home receded slowly. Now, on recent intercontinental flights, there is nothing to see but a sea of cloud beneath the gray metal wingtips. Rushing on or over the earth at fifty, one hundred, or five hundred miles per hour, I have found a special kind of peace akin to the calm of meditation—the paradox of absolute stillness in the midst of rushing movement.

journey

As passengers, there is nothing that we can do except wait until the car stops, the train pulls into the next station, or the plane lands. In essence, we are powerless prisoners, but nevertheless, we can also feel completely free and empowered by the endless universe of possibilities that a journey opens up for us. We have discovered what the eighteenth-century essayist William Hazlitt (1778–1830) called "the soul of a journey," that is, "Liberty, perfect liberty, to think, feel, do just as one pleases."

a pilgrim's

progress

St Helena, a Roman empress in 306 B.C., awaited a physical manifestation of the great faith that had brought her, like many of the millions of pilgrims that have traveled to the Holy Land, on so perilous a journey. Miracualously, divine guidance led the saintly empress to discover the True Cross on which Jesus Christ had been crucified in a cistern near the tomb in which he had been buried. She had the precious relic encased in silver, and built a church to house it over the site of the tomb, now the Church of the Holy Sepulchre, as a focus for future pilgrimages.

In just the same way, though for far less exalted ends, when we travel, we create our own personal shrines and relics. What we anticipate in our destinations is not holiness or divine visions, but something even more miraculous—the opportunity to feel different from the way we feel at home. It is as if the act of traveling to a certain place in the world entitles us to feel happier and more alive. Instead of salvation I want to find new worlds where, to quote Voltaire's Candide, "Things might not be more pleasant, but at least they [and I] would be different."

"The world is before you,
and you need not take it
or leave it as it was when
you came in."

James Baldwin

precon-ceptions

After I graduated from high school, I had time to go on one major trip before going to college in the fall of that year. I chose Mexico as my destination via a few famous landmarks in the U.S. It was clearly absurd of me to attempt to see the whole of the Eastern seaboard in the week I had given myself to travel from New York to the Mexican border. Fortunately, I was not attempting to visit the real United States but wanted instead to experience the imaginary country constructed from events remembered from high school history classes, world-famous tourist attractions, and the locations of movies and television shows enjoyed throughout childhood and adolescence. I had expectations that I had built up of the places I was about to visit and also expectations of how I should feel when visiting them.

By my second day in New York City, I had climbed the Empire State and circumnavigated the Statue of Liberty, visited the Metropolitan Museum and the Guggenheim, and walked from the Bowery to Harlem. I was relieved that I had not been shot at or mugged as all New York "virgins" secretly expect on their first visit. It is more likely that it is the never-ending diet of death and destruction served up by Hollywood and the television companies that is largely to blame for the largely irrational fears that many travelers have.

It would take many subsequent trips finally to rid myself of all the preconceptions that I had and to begin to appreciate this great country in all its variety and grandeur.

"The real voyage of
discovery consists
not in seeking new
landscapes, but in
having new eyes."

"The real voyage of discovery consists not in seeking new landscapes, but in having new eyes."

Marcel Proust

Caye Chaulker is little more than a sandbank with palm trees off the coast of Belizean. The palm-thatched hut was half-built over the water on stilts, with a veranda and a single room within. My hostess was obviously used to the hardier breed of traveler who made it out to the caye to see her. She greeted me from the window of her house and invited me inside. She was making French fries on a portable gas stove for a group of expectant local children. We chatted. She was a forty-five-year-old ex-New Yorker, who had grown tired of the rat race and had wandered south. She had found her island, liked it, and stayed.

She finished making the fries and handed them out to the children. "I do have one luxury," she said, indicating the bed at the back of the hut; it was made with two black satin sheets. I looked around taking in the simple hut, the happy children, and the black satin sheets, and asked myself whether I envied her. How easy would it be to find my own little corner of paradise, build myself a hut, and dream my life away. No, I thought, not now, but maybe when I turn forty-five.

Punta Gorda in Belize was little more than a customs post and a collection of huts built around a jetty. The area's main point of interest, I was told by an fellow traveler, was a river a few miles up the coast with a series of waterfalls. He and some friends were going the next day, and I decided to tag along. We walked along a beach with white sand and palm trees. When the path strayed into the undergrowth, we were pelted with ripe red-and-yellow mangoes falling from the trees, and enchanted by the site of giant tropical blooms. When we reached the river, it was almost too idyllic to be true. We started to follow the stream inland. It was shallow and we could walk along the riverbed to the first falls, which more than lived up to all expectations. About ten feet high, the falls had excavated a deep circular pool some sixteen and a half feet across. We stripped and swam in the cool waters.

We continued up river, finding more waterfalls and pools that got smaller as we got further from the sea. One by one I lost my companions who decided to go no further or to return to Punta Gorda but, driven (as ever) by the desire to see what lay beyond, I continued. The explorer always faces the danger that he may go too far—metaphorically fall off the edge of the earth—and, although no longer interested in the place he is exploring, continues obsessively, because he cannot bear to stop.

The river had become no more than a filet about ten feet wide and a foot deep, overhung with vegetation. I turned a bend and came face-to-face with a Maya family—husband, wife, and two young children—naked as they took a bath in the river. They were of small stature, and with the pudding bowl haircut we associate with Amazonian Indians. The naked Westerner (I was carrying my clothes in a bundle over my shoulder) and the naked Maya family stared at one another across a temporal and cultural chasm. Feeling like an intruder in a world in which I did not belong, I mumbled an apology in Spanish, which they probably did not understand, and withdrew. But I had finally met the Maya whose fabled cities I had come half a world to visit.

lost civilization

I explored Tikal, Yucatan's largest classical Maya site, using a city map drawn by Columbia University. The pyramids and palaces of the Maya are raised on massive earth platforms that have intricately carved facades and roof combs had once been brightly painted. As they had not discovered the arch, the rooms inside those buildings were small, windowless, and oppressively dank. The "palaces" did not have an "inside" as we understand the term. Although the outside was an impressive backdrop for the priests and kings who appeared like actors to their subjects, bedecked in jade, gold, and quetzal feathers, the cramped inner chambers could have been used only as storerooms or dressing rooms.

The Maya are a splendid riddle: centuries of splendor and then nothing. No other culture has left so much physical evidence of their existence and disappeared so completely from human memory—even from that of their own descendants. The ancient Maya could calculate the orbits of the planets and chart the stars with an accuracy not equalled until modern times and counted time in complex calendrical cycles lasting tens of thousands of years. Within a few generations of leaving their cities, they were unaware of urban culture.

The hard-headed answer given by archeologists is that the collapse of the urban Maya was caused by warfare and over-population, combined with sudden ecological disaster. I prefer a more romantic explanation—that they had a sudden change of heart: they took one look at the bloodthirsty gods they had made for themselves and the cities they had built to their glory, and decided that they would be very much better off without them.

sitting in the
seat of

I had to set my watch to wake me up half an hour before dawn so I could see the sunrise from the summit of Tikal's Temple IV, the tallest structure in the Americas until the building of New York's skyscrapers. The building was dedicated in 741 A.D. , the high point of the city's history. The small chamber at the top of the pyramid and its high roofcomb peeked just above the jungle canopy, but the sides of the pyramid were still covered in full-grown trees and shrubs.

kings

As I walked through the jungle along a ceremonial causeway made from stucco twelve centuries earlier for the processions of the god-kings of Tikal, I heard the roar of a jaguar from somewhere close by in the jungle. I hurried on. Even with the ropes put there by the archeologists, it was a challenging climb to the summit of the temple in the pre-dawn grayness. I sat down facing east on the spot where Tikal's priest-kings had watched the sunrise before me. The great red ball of the sun set the eastern sky ablaze, and for a moment the inexorable wheel of time the Maya had so painstakingly charted in their stone calendars seemed to be still.

The physical act of travel can be a slow unfolding of discovery, like the gentle spiritual path to enlightenment taught by the Soto school of Zen, or it can be a sudden realization, full of drama and incident, in the challenging tradition of the Rinzai school.

practicals:
On Foot

Walking

Modern hiking boots have lightweight, yet durable water-resistant uppers, linings made of breathable materials such as Goretex, and thick flexible soles that give you plenty of grip over rough terrain. These give the necessary support for walking over uneven ground.

To improve your stamina and general fitness, whether it be for a sightseeing trip or a more gruelling trek, start by walking at least ten minutes a day, and build up until you are walking a minimum of thirty minutes every day. Walk to work or to the shops instead of driving, and go for a walk in the evening. Take longer walks on weekends, aiming to cover between ten and twelve miles.

practicals:
Public Transport

Buses

In the United States and Europe, bus travel is economical and generally safe. However, in the developing world the combination of poor roads, inadequate safety legislation, and bad driving can be a lethal. When taking a bus in the developing world, find out how many companies cover the route, and evaluate the condition of the bus and driver before making your choice.

Planes

Jet lag is a well-known side-effect of long-haul flights, but less well-publicized is Economy Class Syndrome (ECS). The combination of prolonged immobility, dehydration, and cramped seating in economy class can cause a deep-vein thrombosis—a painful blood clot—in the legs. To reduce the risk, you should avoid tea, coffee, and alcohol (they will dehydrate you) and drink plenty of water during the flight. To prevent cramping, stiffness, and general discomfort, stand up and walk around the cabin once every hour.

Trains

"Eurorail" train passes, entitling the traveler to move freely throughout the European rail network, are available but the service varies significantly from country to country, and there are limitations on the trains that can be used with the pass. Travel passes are also available on Indian railways. If you are traveling second or third class, remember to take bedding with you for longer journeys, as the sleeper bunks are unpadded boards. Travelers in Japan are advised to take a pass for the *Shinkansen* (Bullet train), which is the most convenient and comfortable form of travel connecting the main cities on the island of Honshu. The United States' Amtrak service is slow and has a limited number of routes, but if you are happy with this, they can be great journeys and have a good value monthly travel pass.

practicals:
Private Transport

Cars

In order to drive overseas, you will need to obtain an International Driving Permit in your home country. The permit—a quaint, antique-looking cardboard document—can be obtained by mail from driving clubs and automobile associations, such as the AAA in the United States.

Cycling

On a touring holiday, you might cover about forty to fifty miles a day. If you are a commuter cyclist at best, you will need to train seriously for a cycling trip, with short daily and long weekend training sessions of thirty miles or more for six-to-eight weeks before your departure.

Buy packs that fit on frames over your front and rear wheels, as these provide a far more balanced and a comfortable ride.

If you are traveling to your destination by plane, most carriers will carry your cycle and provide a cardboard packing case free or at a small extra charge. If you are traveling by train or bus to your destination, you can carry your bike in a bike bag that can be used on forms of transport that does not normally allow the carriage of cycles.

chapter 3

right effort: destinations

meditation: "Not to have any desire whatsoever—that is the way." Keizam

If we are to travel at all then we must, to misapprehend Robert Louis Stevenson's famous injunction, "travel hopefully," hoping that we shall find the repose, adventure, or experience that we crave. But expectation is the worst guide to those moments of self-knowledge that are the true gift of travel. The modern traveler is an easy prey to disappointment when the destinations that he or she has journeyed thousands of miles and spent thousands of hard-earned dollars to visit are overcrowded and commercialized packages—holiday "experiences." But should we deny ourselves our dream trip—be it the Louvre or Angkor Wat—for fear that our expectations will be disappointed?

"It is good to have an end to journey toward;

but it is the journey that matters, in the end."

Ursula K. Le Guin

While on a short layover to Delhi, I had decided that the time had come for me to do the "Taj experience," which I had purposely avoided on my previous visit to India. The empty air-conditioned first-class compartment of the 7:15 a.m. Taj Express had none of the chaotic charms of third-class rail travel so vividly brought to life in the Indian leg of Paul Theroux's *The Grand Railway Bazaar*. Arriving at Agra station three hours later, I was greeted, as expected, by a swarm of cycle-rickshaw drivers, who were just as persistent in their attentions as the subcontinent's rich and varied insect life. The monsoon had just broken the long spell of drought in northern India, and western tourists were thin on the ground. I had the pick of the drivers, who competed in offering me the swiftest ride to the Taj. Rightly suspecting that the most persuasive would take me on the most circuitous route, via a succession of souvenir shops, hotels, and restaurants, I walked past them, looking as if I were intent on walking to my destination. The drivers quickly gave up to concentrate their attentions on the Indian passengers exiting behind me.

Several drivers who had not put themselves forward (maybe it was not their turn) sat crouched by their rickshaws on the other side of the street. I approached one, and I told him I wanted to go straight to the Taj. The day was already overcast, and I wanted to get there before the rain started. Even with his careful planning, I had to make one stop at a souvenir shop, where I went through the motions of examining trays of the semi-precious stones and weighty inlaid marble furniture that are the area's main tourist staple. I bought a handful of multicolored gems and a garnet ring as a present for a girlfriend.

Having acquitted himself of his duty to local commerce, my driver took me to the Taj where he deposited me in front of the marble gateway. Just at that moment, there was a tremendous crash of thunder and sheets of water began to fall from a sky turned slate-gray. The only other visitors—a party of local school children—and the many semi-official-looking guards and guides ran for cover. I stood in the gateway and looked at one of the rarest sites in the world: the Taj Mahal as its builder had intended it to be seen, in melancholy solitude.

It was a precious and unexpected gift, but my emotions were mixed at the sight of so famous a building. I remembered the words of another traveler who had come here a century earlier to be made "drunk on the smell of somebody else's work." Of his first vision of the Taj in the 1890s, Mark Twain had written: "You cannot keep your enthusiasms down, you cannot keep your emotions within bounds as that soaring bubble of marble breaks into view. But these are not your enthusiasms and emotions—they are the accumulated emotions and enthusiasms of a thousand fervid writers who have been slowly and steadily storing them up in your heart day-by-day and year-by-year all your life…"

The Taj of a million picture-postcards, travel guides, and tourist videos, floats serenely in an azure sky, reflected in the long rectangular pool that leads the eyes to the tomb flanked by its sentinel minarets. On that early monsoon day, however, the building looked impossibly fragile under the low ceiling of bubbling black and gray clouds, as sheet lightning accompanied by deafening peals of thunder provided the pyrotechnics for an unexpected *son et lumiere*.

Knowing that the rain would not stop for the rest of the day, I walked, soaked to the skin but in blissful solitude, to the mausoleum of Mumtaz Maham. The walls of translucent white marble, inlaid with delicate traceries of semi-precious stones, had been washed clean by the downpour. Sheltering inside were dozens more of the school party I had come across at the entrance. They wore royal-blue shorts and skirts, white shirts, and red bandannas around their necks as bright as the inlays of the walls. They chattered and laughed incessantly. I wondered what expectations they had brought with them to their very own "World Heritage Site," and casting my mind back to school visits, I knew that they were just happy not to be stuck inside doing English or math.

I arrived at the Taj bringing only disdain, but I departed charmed and chastened by an experience so uplifting that it lives in my memory, untarnished like the small chips of Agra carnelian, agate, bloodstone, and tiger's eye that I keep in a shallow dish on my bookshelf.

human weakness

After a three-day journey from Delhi to the former French colonial outpost of Pondicherry, the landscape and people outside the train window had taken on a decidedly sun-baked look to them. As Paul Theroux remarked during his own journey through south India: "After Chingleput, there were no shirts, undershirts disappeared at Villupuram, and further on lunghis were scarce and people were running around in drooping loincloths."

France was the ruling power here until 1954. The cycle-rickshaw driver who picked me up at the station could speak a few words of French. I noted l'Hotel de la Gare flying the French tricolore, where I was later to have an Indo-French meal. But I had come to Pondicherry to wallow in this bubble of Francophonia that had survived two centuries of the British Raj; the main reason for going to Pondicherry was to visit the spiritual community, or ashram, founded by Sri Aurobindo and the Mother in 1926, which now claims a membership of more than two thousand souls, with thousands more devotees in local chapters all over the world. I had great hopes of the ashram, because it long predated the 1970s fashion for all things Eastern, which had seen the Beatles travel to India to study with the Maharishi Mahesh Yogi, and the spread of Indian cults to the West.

The ashram's most ambitious project saw the light of day in 1968, when, with the sponsorship of U.N.E.S.C.O., it founded a utopian city called Auroville seven miles outside of town, endowing it with the following charter:

- Auroville belongs to nobody in particular. Auroville belongs to humanity as a whole.
- Auroville will be the place of an unending education, of constant progress, and a youth that never ages.
- Auroville wants to be the bridge between the past and the present.
- Auroville will be a site of material and spiritual researches for a living embodiment of an actual human unity.

When I visited Auroville, the city of universal peace had a population of around three hundred, mainly Western, residents. I passed several communities but found their inhabitants extremely guarded and unfriendly. When I returned to Pondicherry I made discreet inquiries among the less gaurded members of the Ashram and discovered why. The Mother had died in 1973, creating a power vacuum. While rival factions slugged it out for control, the Aurovillians had made their bid for independence. There followed a long legal wrangle between the Sri Aurobindo Ashram and Auroville, with increasingly dirty tactics.

Instead of finding the spiritual succor I had sought, all I found was an empty personality cult, masking a sordid context for the control of what had become a lucrative business empire.

"I have learned throughout my life as a composer chiefly through my mistakes and pursuits of false assumptions, not by my exposure to founts of wisdom and knowledge."

Igor Stravinsky

belief

A young Western woman in her mid-twenties

prostrated herself in front of the tomb of Sri Aurobindo as if she had been suddenly overcome with grief. She offered a prayer, brought her palms together in front of her face in the Indian salutation of reverence, and then went about her business. I thought how easily we humans give up responsibility for ourselves and not just to other live people, but also to imaginary gods and dead prophets. In Zen, while statues and symbols of the Buddha are accorded respect, there is also a healthy tradition of iconoclasm, as in the story of the Zen monk and the statue of the Buddha. Forced to seek refuge in a temple during a winter storm, the monk had found no kindling to make a fire. Without hesitation, he took one of the sacred images from the altar and burned it to keep warm.

An Australian couple told me about the colossal Buddhas of Bamiyan. They assured me that although it was a terrible two-day trip from Kabul along unpaved roads, it was well worth the effort. The following day I took the bus through the day, arriving in Bamiyan at dusk.

The Colossi that are carved out of the cliff face—the first, one hundred and eighty feet high, the second one hundred and twenty five feet—are the largest images of Buddha in Asia. They were built by the Kushanite rulers of the Bamiyan valley between the fourth and sixth centuries. The hundreds of rock-hewn and painted niches, rooms, and passageways that honeycomb the mountain around the giant images served as monastic cells, prayer halls, chapels, and later as dwellings, once their Buddhist occupants had been swept away by advance of Islam into Central Asia. Defaced on the orders of a Mongol khan in 1221, and eroded by the centuries, the Buddhas spoke only of the folly of men who turn their faith into stone.

icons

the amazing
lakes of Band-e-Amir

The road up to Band-e-Amir runs along unpaved tracks and dry river beds. The five-hour ride on a metal bench in the rear of the open pickup that bounced its way up the foothills of the Hindu Kush more than lived up to the description I had been given. The sun baked my five companions and myself, while the dust thrown up by the truck in front forced us to improvise face masks with whatever item of clothing came to hand. As we climbed to nine and a half thousand feet, the landscape became utterly desolate, with no vegetation to soften the line of crags and cliffs.

In the early hours of the afternoon, we pulled into what looked like a one-horse town in a spaghetti western. A dozen or so single-story mud-brick buildings marked out the settlement's only street, down which a tribesman was riding bareback on a small, emaciated pony. The following day, I would be very grateful to meet a group of such riders when I foolishly decided to walk around the lakes without realizing how large they were, and how easy it was to get lost in an area so devoid of landmarks.

I staggered off the truck, my thighs and buttocks sore from the constant buffeting. I

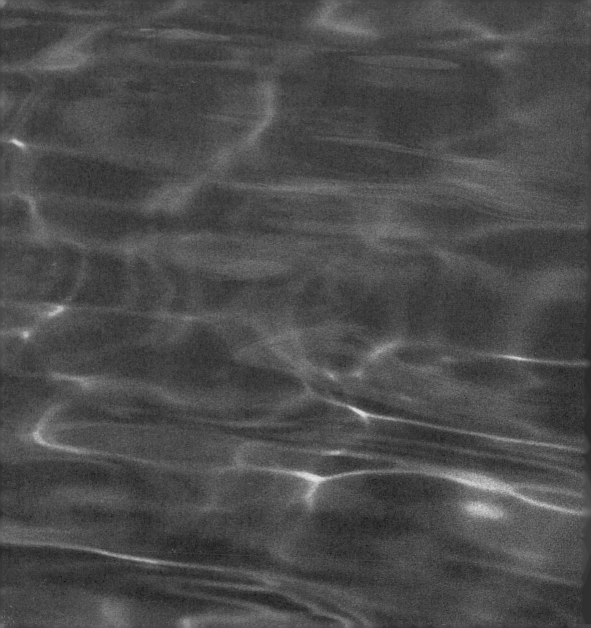

was exhausted, having not eaten or slept properly in the past forty-eight hours, but the sight of clear water cascading over the lip of the dam was so exhilarating that my only desire was to climb up to the side of the first lake.

Credited as miraculous works of Ali, son-in-law of the Prophet, the Dams of the King are in reality natural features, created by the accretion of sulphurous deposits. Divine or natural, Band-e-Amir remains imprinted on my memory as the site of a small personal miracle. I quickly scrambled up to the top of the dam. The view of the lakes was so unexpected that, combined with my weakened physical state, it triggered what I can only describe as an ecstatic trance. The landscape was carved out on an epic scale, and its colors were shocking in their purity: deep cobalt-blue waters met cliffs of red and yellow ochre below a cloudless indigo sky. I lay down on the sandy bank and felt myself dissolve, as if my body were unraveling and mingling with its surroundings. At the same moment, my mind was filled with a sense of profound peace and happiness. After ten or fifteen minutes the feeling began to recede. Still unable to move, I said out loud: "Come! Take me now, for I will never be this happy again."

"If you do not hope,
you will not find what is
beyond your hopes."

St Clement of Alexandria

tourists

"Excuse me" called a voice, "are you American?" No, I replied, "English." The man, a Belgian, explained that the owner of the hostel in Band-e-Amir, where we were staying, had offered him a room in exchange for writing a new tri-lingual menu for his establishment on a cotton sheet. I helped with the English.

As night fell, three brand new sport utility vehicles pulled up on front of the hostel containing a party of a dozen thirty-something French couples fashionably dressed—the men shaved, the women immaculately made up and coiffed. We were first surprised and then annoyed. I had not seen a proper bathroom since leaving India and we were probably as far from civilization as it was possible to go. So how had these "tourists" managed to get here?

The places we visit owe us nothing for the effort we expend to visit them. Despite my twenty-four-hour trip to get there, I had no more right to be there than the French tourists or the Afghani tribesmen who lived there.

"A monk came to Pai-chang and asked, 'What is the most wonderful thing in the world?'

The master replied, 'I sit on top of this mountain.'

Impressed by his words, the monk folded his hands in homage.

Of course, Pai-chang struck the monk with his stick."

Zen saying

traveling
hopefully

The more we offer a place, the less it is likely to deliver. The historical Buddha taught that there is a middle way in all things, and although he would, no doubt, be amused that his distant disciple might wish to apply the vehicle of salvation to so trivial a pursuit as travel, I pray that he would approve. When faced by the macrocosm of the universe or the microcosm of a single place, we must find within ourselves the humility of the pilgrim that both curbs our optimism and corrects our pessimism.

"The map
is not
the territory."

Alfred Korzbyski

practicals: Cities

A popular travel option is the short city-break. A flight and hotel deal is one of the best ways to discover a new city when you have limited time.

- Determine your destination and the best time to visit (know when the city is too hot, overrun by tourists, or shops or attractions are closed). Check for major events: political, sporting, religious, or cultural. Some you may enjoy, some you may wish to steer clear of.
- Think of the city as a huge organic entity with its own rhythms and moods: when does it work, when does it eat, and where does it play? The better you know its customs and habits, the richer your experience will be.
- Hiring a car in some cities is advisable—for example, North American cities—but it would be counterproductive in European cities which are usually congested and have car parking restrictions or pedestrianized zones closed to all traffic.
- Be flexible. Prepare a fallback plan if the attraction you intend to see is closed or too crowded.
- Save your shopping for the last day once you have had a chance to scout the shops in the days before.
- Don't leave your shopping to the airport—some countries have no facilities.

practicals: Nature

- Examine the climate and terrain when planning a trip to the mountains, country, or seaside. These will determine what special equipment you will require for your trip.

- When traveling to south and east Asia , know when the monsoon is due at your destination. This large tropical downpour can cut off major roads, rail links, and the airport in a matter of hours and every year it turns cities all over south Asia into improvized Venices.

- Some subtropical areas are subject to seasonal droughts. In a desert, if you are carrying your own water, count on four gallons of water per person per day.

- Check the snowfall record of the area you are visiting to see if you require special equipment for your car.
- Ensure that your vehicle is completely road worthy and fully equipped with spares before setting off to an isolated area such as a desert or jungle. It is safest to travel with two or more vehicles and always inform someone of your intended route. If you break down, never leave your vehicle. Erect a shelter from the sun, remain with your vehicle until found and, to aid rescue attempts, build three signal fires in the shape of a letter V (the internationally recognized distress signal).

chapter 4

right livelihood: food and lodgings

meditation:

> **"Things don't change, you change your way of looking."** Carlos Castaneda

Have you stopped to wonder at the true meaning of Saint Ambrose's words, "Si fueris Romae, Romano vivito more (When in Rome, do as the Romans do)"? If travel provides the ideal opportunity to derail our thoughts from well-worn patterns by removing us from our day-to-day environment and transporting us to discover new places and make new acquaintances, then, on a very basic level, it also allows our physical selves to escape the routines we have established: feeding, resting, cleaning, exercising, and dressing. When we travel, all these habits are temporarily upset or overturned. Yet, most travelers remain unaware of the changes that are wrought in their physical selves or the impact that these transformations of the body have on the spirit. Depending on how you approach it, experiencing the lifestyles of other cultures can be a challenge, a trial, or a pleasure.

"A student asked his teacher,

'What is the most valuable thing in the world?'

'The head of a dead cat,' the teacher replied.

'Why?' the student asked.

'Because no one can name its price,' was the teacher's reply."

Zen teaching

grand touring

In the eighteenth century, the English gentleman completed his education with a "grand tour" of the continent, which took him to France, Italy, and Switzerland, and back to England via the German principalities. The tour lasted up to two years, during which time the young gentleman, guided by his "bear-leader," as his tutor and companion-come-jailer was unflatteringly known, was supposed to study the language and culture of the countries he visited. To this aristocratic custom, we owe our much devalued modern terms "tourist" and "package tour."

The British have had a long love affair with the landscapes, arts, and architecture of Italy, which according to Dr. Johnson, was the main aim of travel for the grand tourists. "A man who has not been in Italy is always conscious of an inferiority, from him not having seen what is expected a man should see..."

enlightenment in

italy

In 1818 the poet Shelley wrote that there were two Italys:

"...one composed of the green earth and transparent sea, and the mighty ruins of ancient time, and aerial mountains, and the warm and radiant atmosphere which is interfused through all things. The other consists of the Italians of the present day, their works and ways. The one is the most sublime and lovely that can be conceived by the imagination of man; the other is the most degraded, disgusting, and odious. What do you think? Young women of rank actually eat—you will never guess what—garlick!" I count the great poet and the many others who have expressed similar sentiments foolish for claiming to appreciate a country without experiencing the lifestyle of the people who have created the things they claim to admire.

Catastrophe

One day, in Rome, I left my brother's apartment and boarded the bus into the center of town. We were just passing through one of the gates of the ancient walls of Rome when I heard a loud crash: the bus had collided with a van. Although the morning traffic was already heavy, and we were obstructing one of the main thoroughfares that led into the city, the bus driver got off to remonstrate with the van driver and so the passengers all got off and joined in. Soon a crowd of gesticulating Italians had gathered and, after twenty minutes and with gridlock spreading out like the tentacles of an octopus, I decided that I might as well get off and walk to town. As I alighted, I seemed to be the only person interested in the damage that had been caused. I

Curve

went to the side of the bus, but could not even see a scrape. Meanwhile, a police car had pulled up, and the *carabinieri* were alternately attempting to calm things down and being drawn into the fray on one side or the other. Then as suddenly as it had begun, it was all over. The drivers returned to their vehicles, the passengers trooped back onto the bus, the crowd dispersed and we were on the move again.

I believe Italy is one of those countries where things happen to you—not just the visitor but to the natives too. I imagine Italians sailing on the edge of a catastrophe curve, like surfers who just manage to ride on the crest of the wave without, somehow, falling off.

milan

Unlike Sienna, Veronna, Venice, or Florence, which have remained unchanged since the time of the Medici, Milan has undergone major redevelopment, not least during the Fascist period. As the industrial and commerical powerhouse of Italy, it is not a pretty city. Milan does, however, still have the Duomo, the extraordinary white marble cathedral that moved Elizabeth Barrett Browning to write: "How glorious that cathedral is! Worthy almost of standing face-to-face with the snow Alps; and itself a sort of snow dream by an artist architect, taken asleep in a glacier…"

On the day of my visit, it loomed out of the early-morning fog like a gigantic white cruise-liner. As we climbed onto its roof, then sun pierced through the clouds, unshrouding the grimy Milanese cityscape. Frozen, we went for coffee and cakes in the gigantic folly of wrought iron and glass that is the Galleria Vittorio-Emmanuele—surely Europe's first shopping mall—and then on to the only movie that we could all agree to see: *Night of the Living Dead* which, for some unfathomable reason, had been dubbed into French and provided with Italian subtitles.

I was driving a friend's car around the city of Rome, and I took what we thought was a strangely quiet road to the top of the Capitoline hill. No sooner had we arrived on the summit to admire the view than we were surrounded by four police cars that confirmed the motto penned by Geoffrey Harmsworth, a visitor to the Fascist Italy of the 1930s, "In Rome you have to do as the Romans or get arrested." Armed *carabinieri* interrogated us and it took us the best part of half an hour to persuade them that we were tourists who had made a wrong turning. They terrorized us for twenty minutes, finding further violations of the legal code: we had an illegal metal gas can and I was carrying a Swiss army knife in my backpack that they claimed was an offensive weapon. Suddenly they got bored or found something more interesting to do and left us alone and a little dazed.

drama

"Nothing in life is to be feared.
It is only to be understood."

family

The M. family lived in the small northern Italian town of Piacenza. The day started early for the *signora*, who went to the bakers to fetch bread rolls for the family breakfast. We sat down in the dining room for a simple meal of bread, butter, jam, and strong black coffee, after which the *signore*, his children, and I went to work. The *signora* would set out shooping again but, like most Italian matriarchs, she would not dream of shopping in a supermarket. She purchased only raw ingredients from specialist outlets. After shopping and chores, she would spend the rest of the morning preparing lunch.

At one o'clock, the members of the household assembled for an extended midday

values

meal, which consisted of an antipasto—a small appetizer—followed by homemade pasta in sauce, a meat course, vegetables, green salad, and dessert. The evening dinner was a repetition of lunch, but on a much grander scale, with more complicated dishes, sauces, and a fish course introduced between the pasta and meat dishes.

The closeness of the family amazed me. Even though they met for meals three times a day, the conversation was always animated, as if they were meeting after a long absence. It was a culture shock to find myself in a home where family members not only talked, but also communicated.

venice

The landward approach to the lagoon of Venice is not an inspiring one. In the *Great Railway Bazaar*, the passing Paul Theroux penned this little sketch of the view: "Venice, like a drawing room in a gas station, is approached through a vast apron of infertile industrial flatlands, crisscrossed with black sewer troughs and stinking oil, the gigantic sinks and stoves of refineries and factories, all intimidating the delicate dwarfed city beyond."

But once past the factories and refineries (and with the wind blowing the smoke and noxious fumes inland), Venice is magically transformed into the sight that inspired Charles Dickens to write in 1844: "Nothing in the world that you have heard of Venice is equal to the magnificent and stupendous reality. The wildest vision of the Arabian Nights are nothing to the piazza of St Mark, and the first impression of the inside of the church. The gorgeous and wonderful reality of Venice is beyond the fancy of the wildest dreamer. Opium couldn't build such a place, and enchantment could shadow it in a vision."

tradition

The *palazzo* in Venice, where I was staying, was in dire need of repair and was for the greater part an uninhabitable, cold, and damp ruin. My Venetian host was an architect and his family could trace its ancestry back to the fourteenth century. He was fiercely proud of his Venetian pedigree and heritage, and he made me feel quite the Johnny-come-lately, having a family tree that petered out somewhere in the seventeenth century.

Italy may have been united into a single nation-state by Garibaldi in 1861, but I have noticed that many Italians, especially the citizens of the former city states of northern Italy, place loyalty to their cities far above that to their country. After my stay I began to understand why. The towns that I had formerly considered to be well preserved open-air museums—Venice, Florence, Pisa, Veronna, and Sienna—are still thriving communities. Their Italian inhabitants are not annoying interlopers who get in the way of a good day's sightseeing, they are the inheritors and keepers of the traditions that have created these marvels.

"In Italy they seem to have found out how hot their climate is, but not how cold; for there are scarce any chimneys, and most of the apartments painted in fresco; so that one has the additional horror of freezing with imaginary marble."

Horace Walpole in a letter to a friend in 1740

"Enlightenment

is like the moon reflected on

the water. The moon does not get wet,

nor is the water broken. Although its light is

wide and great, the moon is reflected even

in a puddle an inch wide. The whole moon

and the entire sky are reflected in one

dewdrop on the grass."

Dogen

satori

I was wanderinng around the Baths of Caracalla, in Italy. It was still early and I had the ruins to myself. Something began to well up in me and a wonderful, inexplicable sense of complete well being began to electrify my entire body, as if it were physically lifting me off the ground. It felt as though fireworks were going off inside my head, and I began to skip at the sheer joy of it, whooping and laughing with delight as I danced my way through the ruins. The initial feeling of euphoria lasted for maybe ten minutes before receding slowly, but the world was bathed in a rosy glow for several days after.

I have long pondered the meaning of these experiences that have gripped me in the most unlikely of places. I do not think this kind of event is that unusual, but that people are usually too embarrassed or perplexed to discuss their experiences openly unless prompted. A friend of mine, who is of a more conformist religious background, describes a very similar experience as "being touched by an angel." I could have interpreted the experience as an intimation of satori. After all, even among Zen teachers, there is no agreement as to the nature of the experience. For some it is an intensely felt, single event, for others a series of smaller awakenings, that leads to an altered state of consciousness.

"Travel teaches how to see."

African proverb

practicals: Accommodation

Reserving and paying for accommodation in advance leaves the traveler open to disappointment if the glowing descriptions of the travel company or owner does not live up to expectation. If you have prepaid accommodation, you will not only be paying the full official rate for the hotel room or apartment, but also the agent's commission. In many countries, the official advertised rate for accommodation has little to do with the price charged on the spot, which is usually negotiable. Unless you are traveling during a peak holiday period or going to a place hosting a major international event, my experience is that you will be able to find suitable accommodation within your price range without the need to make a firm reservation.

In order to find the best accommodation, you will have to familiarize yourself with your destination and use a guidebook, the Internet, or the national tourist office of the country concerned to decide which area you want to be in. Your destination may also offer types of accommodation available that you may not be aware of, such as government guesthouses, homestays with local families, or love motels!

practicals: Eating

Although you can now find a McDonald's or a Wendy's anywhere in the world, here are a few local alternatives to American-style fast food.

- In Japan, and increasingly in Europe and the U.S., "mechanical" sushi restaurants have brought this food within the poor man's budgets. Sushi on plates priced according to color, ranging from ¥100–¥300 ($1–$3), pass in front of you on a conveyor belt that snakes around the restaurant. You perch on high stools set so closely together that only in Japan are you not instantly on intimate terms with your neighbor. Makisushi—the inspiration of California rolls—are among the cheapest as they only contain pickled vegetables or crabstick; then come egg-sushi (a kind of sweetened omelette) and the cheaper seafood: octopus, salmon, and squid. The priciest sushi includes bonito tuna, prawns, sea urchin, and red fish roe. The Japanese will have a bowl of miso shiru (bean-paste broth) after the meal.

- In Brazil, you buy food by weight. Establishments come in every price range and style of food. You fill up your plate and take it to be weighed on a pair of scales.

- As standard fare in vegetarian south India, a quick meal can be found in station restaurants and cantines everywhere. After paying the two rupiah (four cents) charge at the cash register, you sit at a long communal table. A section of palm leaf is placed in front of you by the waiter, onto which he ladles four hundred grams of white rice. Another waiter appears with a platter of chutneys and pickles. He drops a prescribed, but rather mean, dollop of each condiment on the side of your palm leaf. Using your right hand (as the left is reserved for cleaning up the opposite end of the digestive tract), you scoop rice, flavoring it to taste with the spicy condiments. You leave enough rice to form the base of your dessert, which is made by pouring thin sweetened yogurt into a circular rice trough, which you then eat without trying to lose any of the liquid mush.

practicals: Shopping

Bargaining

Any retail outlet that does not display prices alongside its goods (unless you are in Cartier's, and most likely do not care about the price) should be open to bargaining. While many Westerners feel uneasy about bargaining, it is considered a normal part of shopping in most of the developing world, and should be regarded as a kind of sport, in which the aim is not to acquire goods but to outwit your opponent. Wherever you are or whatever you are buying, the method is the same.

The approach

Even if you have already decided that you are going to buy a particular item, you must appear to be browsing casually. If you give the impression that you actually want what the merchant is selling, he knows that he has you hooked, and then all he has to do is reel you in.

Pick up half a dozen different items, asking the price of some and not others, before you finally pick up the item you have decided to buy. Now examine it carefully. Ask yourself if you really want it, and what you are willing to pay for it. You are now ready to ask how much.

Offers and counteroffers

Generally a merchant will automatically put a markup of anything from one to two hundred percent on his opening price. As it is impossible for you to know what the object is actually worth, you have to decide what it is worth to you. Your first counteroffer should give you plenty of room for maneuvering, so make it at least fifty percent of what you think the goods are actually worth (or how much you are willing to pay for it). A deal can often be clinched at this stage, as the merchant comes down to your desired price after a few rounds of offers and counteroffers, but if he stands his ground, you have to resort to other tactics.

The retreat

Put the goods down and walk away. The seller will usually stop you with an offer. You may wish to ignore this and shop around for five or ten minutes before returning to the shop or stall for round two.

The sale

If the retreat does not do the trick, then you may be pitching your price too low. Convert it into your local currency to see if you are being unreasonable. I have found myself spending half an hour to get a price reduction amounting to no more than fifty cents. The game is fun, but should not be carried to absurd lengths.

chapter 5

meditation: "A good traveler leaves no track." Tao te Ching

When we plan a journey, we entertain ourselves with a slide show of images, culled from television, films, books, and brochures. These will include sights, both natural and manmade, the city streets we will traverse, the museums, beaches, shops, and the eateries we will enjoy. What have we overlooked in this catalog of tantalizing objects? Even if we have chosen to travel alone we will be, at every turn, accompanied by both our fellow travelers and by those who claim our destinations as their homes, and often their livelihoods. As a traveler, I always consider myself to be a guest. And the foremost duty of the guest is to be grateful for the hospitality they receive.

"If a man be gracious and courteous to strangers, it shows he is a citizen of the world, and that his heart is no island cut off from other lands, but a continent that joins to them."

Francis Bacon

accepting differences

Sir Rutherford Alcock, one of the first British diplomats to visit Japan in the latter half of the nineteenth century, wrote "Japan is essentially a country of paradoxes and anomalies where all—even familiar things—put on new faces and are curiously reversed." He gave examples: "They write from top to bottom, from right to left, in perpendicular instead of horizontal lines; and their books begin where ours end..." In their customs he found them perplexingly contrary.

There is no awareness in Alcock of the extraordinary impression he himself must have made on his hosts. He was too busy cataloging the inexplicable contradictions of the "natural" (that is, British) way of doing things, to realize that his own dress, personal habits and worldview were quite outlandish to the Japanese. Neither did the experience inspire him to reflect on his own ways, nor look beyond the superficial differences of custom and dress to the shared human experience beneath.

"I look upon every day to

be lost, in which I do not

make a new acquaintance."

Dr. Johnson

aliens

Until the early 1990s, visitors to Japan were asked to present their passports under a sign that read "Aliens." The word was chosen to convey the Japanese "gaikokujin" (foreigner, literally, "person from outside the country"). In the early years of my stay, as I waited in line for my passport to be stamped each time I returned to Japan, I would wonder whether the word referred to the disembarking passengers or to the nation that awaited on other side of passport control.

calligraphy

My calligraphy teacher, Kimura-san, was dressed conservatively in a plain gray skirt and matching sweater. We had met by chance and when I told her that I was in Kyoto to study Japanese she invited me to visit her calligraphy school. My Japanese was still rudimentary, and her spoken English little better, so verbal communication was labored, and we quickly resorted to the vocabulary of gesture, posture, and facial expression when we could not convey our meanings through speech.

My first lesson began. She instructed me to kneel in front of one of the low tables that were the classroom's only furniture. The floor had recently been recovered with new *tatami* mats, which were soft and pale gold in color and smelled of freshly-cut hay. She laid out in front me the tools of the calligrapher's trade. "These are for you," she said. "They are a present from me."

I was overjoyed, like a boy who has just been handed a toy that exceeds all his expectations on Christmas morning. Her gift consisted of a black felt pad on which to rest the paper and a long metal paperweight the size of a school ruler to hold it in place; an inkstick and inkstone; a small white-and-blue porcelain water pitcher; a light green porcelain brushrest in the shape of a dragon; and, finally, three bamboo and bristle brushes. She then showed me several types of paper: cut sheets of a stiff yellowish practice paper, which, she said, could be substituted with newspaper; and then the rolls of fine rice paper for display—some pure white and smooth, others creamy ivory colored and textured.

A Western calligrapher uses a bottle of ready-made China ink, but the Japanese calligrapher has to make their own ink by grinding the inkstick on the inkstone. The ritual of ink-making is an essential part of the preparation for calligraphy, as it gives one time to settle and center one's mind on the task ahead; it also allows the calligrapher to decide on the density of the ink, which he can vary according to the paper he intends to use.

Kimura-san was kneeling beside me in the formal seiza kneeling position, which is hard on the ankles of Westerners who are more used to slouching in chairs than sitting on hard floors. She, on the other hand, looked completely at ease.

"I will show you," she said. From that moment until the end of the demonstration she was completely absorbed by the task at hand. She placed the inkstone in front of her, precisely parallel to the edge of the table. The smooth black

stone had a low rim and a reservoir at one end. She poured a small amount of water onto the stone and picked up the inkstick. It was unused and still in its paper wrapping. She unwrapped it, revealing a series of gold characters etched into its surface. Holding the inkstick in the thumb and two fingers of her right hand and the inkstone with her left hand, she dipped the stick into the water and ground it in circular motions on the stone. The stick dissolved and a thin fillet of black sumi ink flowed into the reservoir, darkening it with every turn. Depending on the quantity and density of the ink one desires to make, the process can take from five to fifteen minutes. In addition to helping one relax, grinding the ink is also meant to strengthen the fingers of the hand and thus improve control of the brush.

Having made the desired quantity of ink, Kimura-san dried the inkstick and placed it to one side. She put a piece of practice paper on the felt pad and held it in place with the paperweight. She selected a medium-sized brush, holding it in with the thumb and two fingers of her right hand, so it was vertical over the paper. She took a deep breath, and for my benefit, indicated that she was breathing from her *hara*—a spot about two inches below the navel which is considered to be the center of the human body in traditional Chinese and Japanese medicine. She dipped the brush into the ink and with complete assurance wrote a series of kanji (characters) on sheet after sheet.

Now it was my turn. I ground the inkstick with a figure-of-eight motion on the stone. The tip of the new brush was stiff with glue and I had to soften it in some water before it could be used. Inexpertly, I loaded it with ink. After witnessing her effortless demonstration, I felt like complete oaf. I took a deep breath from my *hara* before I attempted to write the first stroke of the character *ame*, meaning rain. *Ame* is built up of eight separate strokes, which cannot be written at random but in order; the shape and heaviness of the line and serifs are determined by the style of the character, and realized by the calligrapher's manipulation of the density of the ink, and absorbency of the paper, and the pressure applied to the brush.

My first "ame" looked as if it had been left out in the rain. I had used too much ink and pressed too hard on the paper, making large blotches instead of clean straight lines with rounded ends. For my second attempt, she knelt behind me and held my brush hand with hers. I could feel her body lightly pressed against my back, and my posture changed to imitate her: my shoulders relaxed, my neck and back straightened, and I felt more centered.

Her touch was light on my hand but firm. She guided the brush into the ink and back over the page and drew the central hooked vertical line of the four-stroke character for water. The brush lifted and came down to the right of the vertical to create the left-hand element, and then the two right-hand elements. In those few seconds she had succeeded in conveying to me just a little of what it was like to be a calligrapher of twenty five year's experience. I had learned the difference between writing Japanese and the art of calligraphy and had received my first lesson in living Japanese Zen.

"There are many wonderful things,
and nothing is more wonderful than man."

Sophocles

Manners

It was my first invitation to a Japanese friend's house. I knocked on the door that opened into my host's Western-style kitchen where she and several others were sitting on chairs around a kitchen table. The floor was wood, and the whole arrangement looked as un-Japanese as I could imagine or had expected. Without thinking, I stepped in with my shoes on. To this day, I can remember the look of horror on their faces as they chorused "shoes!" There was no polite amusement or understanding, but only shock that I could have made so elementary a mistake.

Although I had metaphorically taken off my shoes on the day of my arrival in Japan, I had to acquire the habit of taking off my shoes when entering a Japanese home, the hard way.

"If your mind is empty, it is always ready for anything; it is open to everything.

In the beginner's mind there are many possibilities; in the expert's mind there are few."

Shunryu Suzuki

my house

I wanted to live in the kind of surroundings that the English potter Bernard Leach had experienced on his visit to Japan in 1953. He described it as "Voiceless beauty; the almost empty room, the exquisite adjustment of things, the color of the green tea in its bowl, the lie of the chopsticks on their rest, the writing on the wall of the recess, the white light through the paper shoji, and the shadow of bamboo leaf upon it. I could go on indefinitely but it has to be lived to be really felt."

Unfortunately, my arrival in the country coincided with the beginnings of the "bubble" economy—a roller coaster economic boom based on inflated land and share prices that came to a crashing end in 1993. At one time in the late 1980s, any undistinguished neighborhood in Tokyo was notionally worth more than the whole of the island of Manhattan. Anyone owning property found that they were millionnaires overnight, with access to huge sums of cheap credit. All over Japan, people were tearing down their traditional wooden houses, which froze in the cold winters and sweltered in the hot, humid summers, and replacing them with centrally heated and air-conditioned concrete-and-glass "mansions."

During my time in Japan, all the traditional Japanese houses I visited and stayed in invariably belonged to foreign residents. This did not mean that the Japanese had abandoned their lifestyle in favor of our own—far from it. They still lived at floor level, took off their shoes indoors, and washed outside their baths—they had merely upgraded their building materials, furniture, and plumbing.

Several weeks after my arrival, I met Vince from Pittsburgh, who was the first American to study for his undergraduate degree at the Law Faculty of Kyoto University. He told me that he knew someone with a room to rent in a "typical Japanese house," but that she was

French and not Japanese. "Her name is Yvonne. She runs a French restaurant in Higashiyama," Vince said. We arranged to go to the restaurant that evening.

Higashiyama, a residential area to the northeast of the center, was not where you would expect to find a French restaurant. Judging from its layout, Chez Yvonne's had once been a neighborhood bar. It had a long counter, behind which Yvonne did all the cooking, with seats at the counter and a small seating area beyond it with a few tables.

"Irrasshai! (You are welcome!)," Yvonne called out the traditional Japanese greeting to customers, as she heard the sliding door open. We were the first customers, and she was standing behind the counter, peeling potatoes to make the french fries for which her restaurant was famous. Although neither tall nor particularly overweight, Yvonne projected a larger-than-life image. In this country of quiet, modest, reserved people, she was brash, loud, and outspoken. She hailed from Cannes in the south of France, and had come to Japan in the '60s after falling in love with a Japanese jazz musician. Although they never married and were now separated, Yvonne had not only managed to stay in Japan but had also opened a restaurant.

Yvonne and I hit it off at once. Vince told her that I was looking for a room, and she told me that she had one to rent in her house. It was agreed that I would come to see it the next day.

Yvonne's house was on the northwestern side of Kyoto, not far from the Kamo river. It was everything that a Japanese house should be: It was made of wood, of course, all the internal partitions were paper-covered "shoji," and the floors were "tatami" throughout. The kitchen, which is considered to be part of the outside in a Japanese house, had a beaten-earth floor and opened onto an inner courtyard which contained all the sanitation

the
house
provided: a
hose pipe with
cold water to wash
with, and a cesspit toilet. I
was glad that the icy Kyoto
winter was over, but the absence of
a bathroom was easy to explain and
excuse, as there were several "sento" (public
bathhouses) in the neighborhood. If there is one
thing that I miss about Japan now, it is the scalding
Japanese bath—taken in the deep square tubs at home, in
public bathhouses, and in "onsen," or hot spring resorts, that are
found all over this volcanic archipelago.
I was learning Japanese and living in a traditional Japanese house, but
I knew almost nothing of the modern Japan that was then challenging the
United States for economic supremacy. That discovery lay in the years ahead, and
in a series of experiences that first showed me all the differences between
our ways of life, but later led me to appreciate how, beneath these
superficial differences, all the members of the human family are identical.

"What we call 'I'
is just a swinging door
which moves when
we inhale and exhale."

Shunryu Suzuki

cele

brate!

We in the West have our great pageants and processions—like the St. Patrick's Day parade in New York—but what we have lost and still survives in Japan is the neighborhood festival. In Tokyo's shitamachi (literally, the lower city, that is, the working class district), every shrine holds its own matsuri. The young men (and increasingly the young women) of the area change into hapi coats, wear headbands, and take turns at carrying the heavy gilded o-mikoshi (portable shrines) around their streets, shouting "Wasshoi! Wasshoi!" to sustain their spirits, frighten away evil spirits, and reaffirm their sense of belonging. They have a sense of community that, although it can still be found in small town America, has long vanished from larger cities.

"There is a great difference between traveling

to see countries or to see people."

Emile Jean-Jacques Rousseau

practicals: Gift Giving

The act of gift giving is charged with social meaning that can easily wrongfoot the best-intentioned giver, causing grief and upset when only kindness was intended. In the West gifts are given to mark end-of-year holidays and rites of passage, such as birth, graduation, and marriage, but in many cultures of Africa and the Asia-Pacific, gifts are part of a system of "ceremonial exchange" that defines and cements social relations both between individuals, families, and organizations.

In Japan, one of the world's most finely tuned systems of gift exchange operates on set dates throughout the year, as well as on specific occasions such as a return from trips abroad, marriages, births, and funerals. When visiting colleagues or friends in Japan, the best gift to bring with you is a typical product from your home country, for example tea from the UK or wine from California. The value of the gift should not exceed $25–$50, as a more expensive gesture would embarrass your hosts, and force them to repay you by purchasing an expensive gift. Sometimes gifts are not offered immediately and the obligation can be stored up for repayment in the future.

practicals : Language

One of the greatest limitations on travelers is language. Denied this basic human faculty, they are forced to rely on nonverbal communication, whose basic signs, they would like to think, they share with the whole human race. Such an assumption is usually unfounded: a forward nod of the head is commonly held to meet "yes," and side-to-side motion, "no," but these interpretations are not universal. In certain cultures the two actions are reversed and in others, subtle semantic nuances are introduced so that, in certain constructions, "yes" can imply a negative, and "no" an affirmative.

A phrasebook can be of very little practical use. Even if you can manage the pronunciation of the word or phrase, you will not find the reply easy to understand or in your phrasebook. Of slightly more use is a visual phrasebook, which provides photographs of hotels, restaurants, and airports, common items, as well as activities such as changing money and shopping.

When traveling to an area whose language and script are completely unknown, the only linguistic preparations I can recommend are to learn the written and spoken forms of the numbers, from one to ten, and the six words that are the basis for all human interaction: "yes, no, hello, goodbye, please," and "thank you."

chapter 6

right concentration: memories

meditation: "The mind should be nowhere in particular." Takuan

In Zen Buddhism, an individual personality does not exist. It is deemed to be an illusion with no more solidity than a shifting sandbank constantly remolded by the currents of time and space. If there is anything at all that can be described as a permanent self, then it is composed in the act of remembering, and in the value that we place on our past experiences. But what are those memories composed of? Are they the faithful record of lived events, or merely personal fictions, created from imagination, history and hearsay, that we have fashioned into shackles that bind our former ways of thinking and being?

"Memories are hunting horns

whose sound

dies on the wind."

Guillaume Apollinaire

remembrance
of things past

The French nineteenth-century novelist Marcel Proust constructed his most important work, *A la Recherche du Temps Perdu*, around a personal vision of time and memory. The slightest detail of every moment we have ever lived, he believed, is stored within us waiting to be resurrected by a chance event that brings together the streams of past and present. In a passage at the beginning of the first volume, the narrator suddenly recovers his lost childhood when he tastes a madeleine sponge cake dipped in tea.

Although Proust's ideas have always fascinated me, I do not recognize the unbroken stream of memory that he describes as being in my own life. In my experience memory is episodic and discontinuous. In order to make it into a continuous stream of narrative, we, like Proust, have to fill in the gaps with hearsay, such as those family anecdotes told and retold on occasions by relatives who invariably start, "You must remember the time when you…"

"There are many people who mistake their imagination for their memory."

Josh Billings

memories

One of my most enduring childhood memories of my vacations is of the end of the six-foot-long stuffed saltwater crocodile that had been brought back from French Indo-China by my great-great-grandfather. It hung on a couple of nails on a beam in the attic, glaring toothily at generations of Chaline children. At least once every summer, the hapless reptile was taken for an annual outing to the river, where my father and uncle, ever fond of a practical joke, would tow it behind their canoe, shouting "Au secours! (Help!)" at the top of their lungs and paddling for all they were worth. After several years of this treatment, the unfortunate beast finally began to decompose and fall apart. As a fitting warrior's farewell to the old sea-salt, we children built a pyre in the garden around which we danced until the carcass was entirely consumed.

river of life

The smoke from a burning crocodile—a pyre made when I was a child—mingles in my memory with that of another many thousands of miles away. I had gone to Varanasi (formerly Benares) to witness one of the age-old rituals of death in India: cremation on the banks of the Ganges.

Although the sun had not yet dawned when I left my hotel, the streets were already crowded. I followed the pilgrims down toward the three miles of stone ghats (steps) that front the river at Varanasi. They come every year by the tens of thousands to bathe in the sacred waters of the Great River, or Borra Ganga, as the Ganges is known to the Hindus, whose powers are described in the epic poem, The Ramayana, in the following verses: "Those, who through the curse, have fallen from heaven, having performed ablutions in this stream, become free from sin; cleansed from sin by this water and restored to happiness, they shall enter heaven and return to the gods."

I was still several hundred yards from the river when I spotted a funeral procession several streets away on a parallel course to the river. I had been warned not to get too close to a funeral procession and never to take photographs. A dozen or so mourners followed the corpse carried on a stretcher. It was wrapped in a white shroud on which had been scattered garlands of red and yellow flowers. There was little solemnity to the occasion. The mourners had to jostle their way past pilgrims and hawkers; they alternated between wailing their grief and shouting at passersby to clear the narrow alleyways. I reflected on how we in the West have succeeded in almost abolishing disease and aging. We have forgotten what the grinning face of death looks like, which is hidden away in hospitals and hospices; and corpses are quickly collected, embalmed, and disposed of.

Our separate courses finally reached the river, wide as an inland sea at Varanasi—vast enough to give the pilgrims an intimation of the eternity of Brahma. I was standing about fifty yards from the funeral party. I watched in morbid fascination as the body was laid out on a wooden pyre. The officiant, who might have been a priest or the deceased's senior relative performed the final rites over the body. A moment later, he set light to the pyre. Whether the wood was soaked in a combustible material or just dry from the summer heat, it erupted instantly into a fierce blaze. The light cotton shroud was consumed first, momentarily revealing the body it had hidden from view before it, too, was engulfed by the flames. A pillar of dense black smoke rose into the air, but fortunately the wind blew it away from me.

As I watched, I was transported again half a world and several centuries away, to a time and place I had witnessed in a very different kind of death. The Houston Cancer Center is the most advanced facility of its kind in the world. It was the last time I saw my mother alive. She was unrecognizable from the combined effects of the tumor that had taken over a large part of her body and the massive doses of chemotherapy that had failed to control it.

A few months later I was going down to the Loire, in France. Along with my relatives, I was not accompanying a body, but an urn that contained my mother's ashes. She had been cremated in the United States, and my stepfather had smuggled her ashes back to France for a family funeral. We made a strange party, my brother and I, uncles, aunts, and cousins, congregated on the river bank early on Sunday morning to fulfil my mother's wish to be scattered in the river. As it is illegal to dispose of a body in this way, we had had to wait until the morning after the funeral. It was mid-summer, and the water level was unusually low. Instead of climbing down and across the dry riverbed to the deeper central channel where the water still flowed, we decided to throw the ashes off the middle of the bridge.

In Varanasi, the pyres burn for several hours before the bodies are completely consumed, and then the ashes are thrown into the river. I turned away from the cremation and watched the brown waters of the Ganges, swollen by distant monsoon rains. The pilgrims stood waist deep in the water

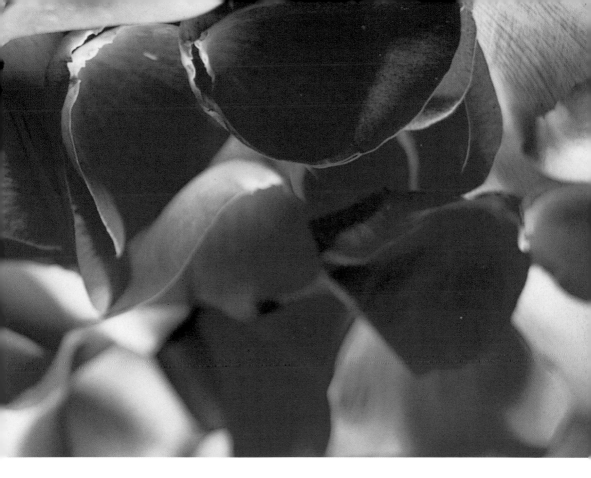

performing their sacred ablutions as they prayed facing the sun. The bloated body of a dead cow came floating past, revolving slowly in the current. I had not brought any of my mother's ashes with me, but I consigned her memory to the holy waters, hoping that she had, at last, found repose.

One
New Year's Day,
Master Ikkyu carried a
human skull attached
to the end of a bamboo
pole through the streets
of Kyoto, shouting
"Beware! Beware!"

When the townspeople reproached him and complained that he was a killjoy, he replied, "Death should not spoil your celebrations."

altered reality

Photographers spend hours staging their shots so that, like painters, they interpret reality and not, as is often believed, merely reproduce it. Even landscape photographers have their tricks—a selection of lenses, film types, and light filters to choose from—to achieve their results. Like them, we can edit our memories, whether consciously or subconsciously, and rethink or refeel them as we want to. And yet, in the background, there are images which linger on mostly unnoticed until something acts as a trigger that brings them to the foreground.

Time passes,

There is no way

We can hold it back.

Why, then, do thoughts linger

Long after everything else is gone?

Ryokan

My favorite souvenirs

tend to be tangible and personal reminders of a particular experience or event. A few of them can pass muster as *objet-d'art* and can be displayed for their aesthetic or conversation-starting qualities, but most have ended up in an old wooden toy chest the size of a small traveling trunk. For me, investigating the depths of the chest for the first time in many years, it is like sinking a bore-hole into the strata of my own past.

"An unexamined life is not worth living."

Socrates

on my mind

I pull out the poncho I bought in a covered market in Mexico's second city, Guadalajara. I am glad the strong smell of goat is almost gone, though enough of it remains to take me back to the narrow alleyways of the market. I bargained hard for two days to get the poncho, along with a white sweater.

A folded piece of paper falls out of the poncho. When I unfold it I read the painstakingly handwritten lyrics of an Irving Berlin song, "Harlem on My Mind." As I read, I can hear the crackly period accompaniment, and Ethel Walters's soulful delivery that captures the bittersweet realization of the woman who has everything except the thing she truly desires which is always out of reach.

"Writing is learnt
from letters, but
Nature from land to
land. One land,
one page."

Paracelsus

chasing
waterfalls

Memories cascade into one another, combining real events with fictions, creating anchors to past selves that we must sever if we are to not be stranded by them like ships left high and dry at low tide. Our memories do not define us. Like the luggage the returning traveler has finished with, they should be unpacked and stored away—out of sight and out of mind—and not carried around to weigh us down.

practicals: Journals

As a writer, I am fascinated by writing materials, and whenever I go to a new country, one of the first things I do is buy a set of local writing materials—pens, brushes, inks, notebooks, paper—that I will use to keep a travel journal or jot down ideas. Scrapbooks may appear childish, but they often provide the most touching and personal reminder of a trip. Again, find a suitable notebook during your holiday and keep an eye on materials to include, such as pamphlets, brochures, and tickets to tourist attractions.

practicals:

The writing of the postcards is an enjoyable ritual that I usually tackle on the second or third day of the trip, often after breakfast with a contented stomach and a view to inspire me. I will write letters on longer trips of a month or more. But postcards and letters are increasingly being superseded by email. While it is difficult to transport your computer and your email settings, you will now find Internet cafés from Dallas to Delhi. All you require is an

Keeping In Touch

account with a universal mail provider, such has Hotmail or Yahoo, which can be retrieved from any terminal in the world, as all you need to remember is your user name and password to access your account. Of course, the annoying thing about this form of correspondence is that it could be sent from anywhere in the world. And I will miss not receiving the trashy, dog-eared postcards with terribly designed stamps.

chapter 7

right attention: precautions

meditation:

"We should find perfect existence through imperfect existence." Shunryu Suzuki

Although travel is safer and more comfortable than it has ever been, it is, by its very nature, a risky enterprise. The more you travel, the more you are likely to experience delay, accident, theft, and illness. Although their impact can be minimized by taking the proper practical precautions—medical, loss, and cancellation insurances—their inconvenience can never be avoided altogether. To this Buddhism has two answers. On the superficial level, it teaches that attachment to material objects is one of the key sources of suffering. Carry your possessions lightly, and their loss will not drag you down. On a deeper level, it will teach you that what makes you unhappy is not the inconvenience or loss itself but your expectation that everything should have gone without a hitch.

A Zen master lived in a hut deep

One evening when he was out, a thief came to his hut. The man quickly found that there was nothing to steal. The master returned and surprised him. "You have come a long way," he said, "and you should not leave

in the forest.

empty-handed. Take my clothes." The bewildered thief took the clothes and ran away. The master sat naked looking at the moon. "Poor fellow," he said, "I wish I could have given him this beautiful moon."

una casa de

The taxi had dropped me off at the base of the volcano. I was in Central America, in Atitlan, Guatemala, but the entire area had an unmistakenly Alpine look—as long, that is, as you ignored the gigantic cones of active volcanoes that are not a noted feature of Swiss or north Italian scenery. The similarity had struck Aldous Huxley, who had visited the area in 1934. On seeing Lake Atitlan, he wrote: "Lake Como, it seems to me, touches the limit of the permissibly picturesque; but Atitlan is Como with the additional embellishment of several immense volcanoes. It is really too much of a good thing."

confianza

I had come to Atitlan to see its three active volcanoes. The lava here, however, does not flow dramatically like torrents of bright molten metal, it inches its way down the grassy slope like giant black caterpillars, devouring the landscape at leisure. During the day, one sees nothing more dramatic than steaming piles of black rubble, like gigantic cowpats. I realized that I would have to wait until dusk to see the flows glowing all the way from the summit and down the slopes, but was resigned to missing this sight, as I was on a tight schedule and had arranged for the taxi to return to pick me up in the late afternoon.

When I made my way to our agreed meeting place, there was no car to be seen. I climbed back up the slope to make sure that I had not made a mistake and that the car was not waiting further along the slope, but the unpaved track was deserted in both directions. I had not seen so much as a car, van, or bus in the area since morning, and as far as I knew, there were no towns in the immediate vicinity where I could find either a hotel for the night, or a bus or a taxi to take me back to the capital. Cursing my foolishness, I set off along the path that cut diagonally uphill, hoping that it would lead me to a village. I looked back up the mountain, and caught the faint glow of the lava flows as the light began to fade. At least I was going to see the sight I had come over thirty miles to see.

I walked for about half an hour without encountering a soul. I went on—paths, after all, have to lead somewhere, and this one had a well-trodden look about it. I was fast getting used to the idea that I might have to walk through the night, when I saw a solitary figure approaching in the other direction. At first, I admit that I was a little worried. I was in the middle of nowhere, in a country not always reputed for its love of foreigners. As the person drew nearer, I was relieved to see that it was a farmer coming from his fields, a hoe on his shoulder. He was dressed like an extra from *The Magnificent Seven*: cotton smock, trousers, and poncho, though without the wide-brimmed sombrero. I half-expected him to ask me to come and rescue his village from bandits. He seemed just as surprised and disquieted as myself at meeting a stranger on his path.

"Por favor, senor, Hay un hotel cerca de aqui?" (Is there a hotel near here), I asked.

He looked at me uncomprehendingly. But my plight must have been clear to him. He replied but it took several repetitions for me to understand. "Conozco a una casa de confianza" (I know a trustworthy household). He spoke Spanish but with such a strong accent it made me think that it was not his first language.

After a rather labored exchange, I understood that we were not far from his village. I put myself into his hands, and he led me back along the way I had come and up along a side path that I had earlier discounted. The first thing I saw as we climbed up to the brow of the hill was a large rusty sign that read: "Bebe Coca Cola." There was no road, no electricity, but the power of corporate capitalism was omnipresent. The first houses of the village were just beyond the sign. I say houses, but they were little more than large huts with mud walls and thatched roofs.

As we approached, the village's bush telegraph must have gone into overdrive because families were stepping out of their houses to greet me as I passed, and when I reached the "center" of the village a few moments later, I was received by a reception committee composed of several old men and a young woman in her twenties who spoke unaccented Spanish and some English. She introduced herself as the local schoolteacher. It was lucky that I had arrived that day, she said, as she only came to the village one day a week. This made me wonder as to what my reception would have been if she had not been present.

Surrounded by close to the entire population of the village, I explained my situation to the schoolteacher. My arrival was obviously the biggest thing that had happened around here since the last revolution, or, at least, since they'd put up the Coke sign. My hopes of returning to civilization were quickly dashed. There was a bus to the local market town that ran along a road that passed a few kilometers away from the village, but there were no more until the next morning. No one in the village owned a car or truck. There was nothing to do but walk on or stay for the night. The schoolteacher consulted with my rescuer and the village elders.

The village did have a general store of sorts—though tin shack would have been a better description—which sold the few luxuries these people could afford: Coca-Cola, not surprisingly, some dry goods, cigarettes by the item rather than by the packet, and bags of great pink and white marshmallows. I bought a packet of biscuits, which I handed out to the local children who now formed a cordon around me.

The discussion ended, the schoolteacher came to tell me that she had found somewhere for me to stay. I was led to a hut like all the others. It consisted of two rooms with beaten-earth floors. The outer room was obviously the kitchen and living space, as it contained the cooking hearth and the family's few stores and possessions. The smaller inner room contained only a raised sleeping pallet covered in woven reed mats which was roughly the size of a Western double bed. My hosts were a family of six.

"Where will they sleep?" I asked, as it was clear that I was taking their only bedroom. "They will be all right, don't worry," the teacher said. "But they would appreciate something for their trouble." "Will this be enough?" I asked producing a ten-quetzal note.

The sum I profered was probably equal to a week's

earnings for the head of the household. He took the note, and it immediately disappeared into the recesses of his clothing. The family made their beds for the night in their kitchen, and I was left to settle as best I could with a rather grubby blanket and straw mat. I managed to fall asleep, but awoke several hours later itching from my ankles and wrists. I was being eaten alive by some kind of blood-sucking parasite that was attracted to those parts of the body where the skin was thinner (and warmer) and the blood easiest to obtain. Unable to sleep, I sat up for the rest of the night fending off further attacks as best I could. At dawn, I got up, carefully picked my way around my hosts, who were still fast asleep in a huddle, and hurried down to the road where I had been told the bus ran.

adventure

Losing one's way has always been one of the major hazards of travel. Although it can prove fatal in the harsh and unforgiving environments of the jungle or the desert, in gentler inhabited landscapes, it is merely inconvenient. I was lost on the slopes of Atitlán in Guatamala when my taxi, which had dropped me off, had failed to come back to collect me as I had requested. I was not unduly worried. I calculated that I could be no more than twelve miles from the nearest town, I had enough clothes to keep out the evening chill, and a few supplies. I consoled myself with G.K. Chesterton's words that

"An adventure is

only an inconvenience rightly considered."

"Heaven-sent calamities you may stand up against,

but you cannot
survive those
brought on by
yourself."

Shu Ching

feeling better

The most common affliction the Western traveler succumbs to in the developing world is stomach trouble which rejoices in such names as "Montezuma's revenge" and the "Delhi belly." One afternoon in Chichicastenango in Guatamala, I developed a high fever accompanied by bouts of vomiting and diarrhea. Tom, my travelling companion, who was a second-year medical student, diagnosed typhus. On the second day with no change in my condition it became cholera, and on the third, hepatitis. His diagnostic skills left a lot to be desired. My fever broke on the evening of the third day and, although weak, I was recovered enough by the next morning to continue the journey. I decided that I must have had one bad banana in a bunch I'd had for lunch. Although, as Susan Sontag has said, "Everyone who is born holds dual citizenship, in the kingdom of the well and in the kingdom of the sick." The traveller to the developing world has a V.I.P. pass to the latter.

"Patience

is the best remedy

for every trouble."

Plautus

New Year

As I withdrew my money from the hotel safe in Salvador de Bahia, Brazil, I chatted to the hotel receptionist about my New Year plans. I explained that I was staying in Barra for the celebrations to which she replied, "Oh no...much too dangerous." I had already been warned by a friendly security guard to "be careful" and not to wear an expensive watch, jewelry or carry a wallet with me into town or to the beach.

Like Carnaval, New Year is a great popular celebration in Brazil. The wealthy give lavish parties in their villas and yachts, and the poor throng the streets and beaches, drinking and dancing to the free music that is always on offer. I had been led to expect chaos, violence, and danger, but I found the event had been well organized. Squads of fearsome-looking and feared military police were on duty at key points and although I did see trouble—a particularly short and nasty fight between two groups of youths—the police were there in seconds and the participants had disolved into the crowd.

"Do not seek
the truth.
Only cease to
cherish opinions."

Zen saying

the human animal

Humans are only one of the animal dangers the traveler is exposed to.

Until
I went on Safari in Africa, I never
really questioned the Disney-inspired view that
wild animals were humans in cuddly-fur suits, each with
their characteristics: lions were brave and noble; elephants,
placid and kind; hyenas, wily and cowardly; and so on—but when
I came face-to-face with the real thing, I realized that animals were
just animals. Lions are either fed or hungry; elephants are best left alone
(a rogue male flattened a car during my visit to the Kruger National Park
in South Africa, and had to be shot) and a hyena will snap your leg off
as soon as look at you.
The most frightening animal on earth, however, is neither lion nor even shark.
When I went on my first dive on Australia's Great Barrier Reef, I asked the
instructor, trying to hide the anxiety in my voice, "Will I see any sharks?" "Only
if we're very lucky," she replied.
Sharks may take a bite out of the occasional swimmer, but that is
nothing to the wholesale slaughter of sharks that takes place in the
oceans of the world on a daily basis. On the Great Barrier
Reef, sharks have become an endangered species.
The most frightening animal on earth, is, of
course, the human animal.

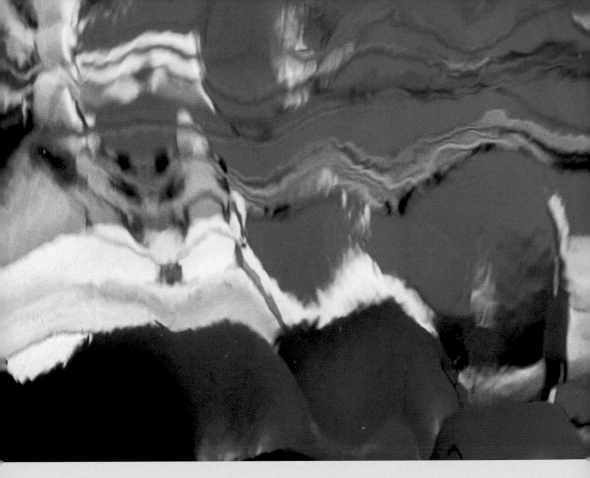

"Life is a great bundle of little things."

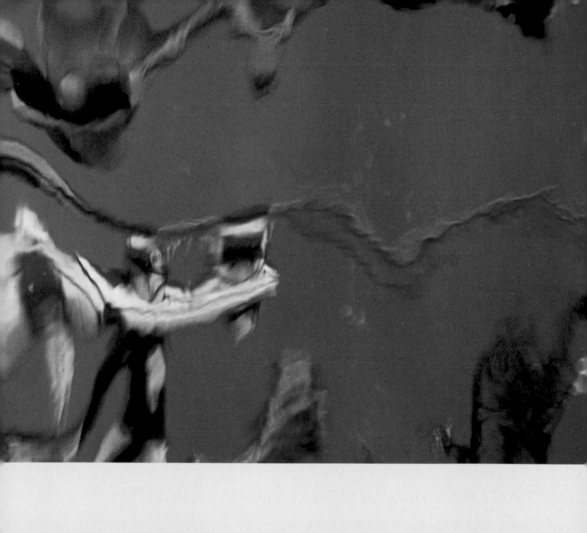

I have only fallen seriously ill twice on my travels.

Resigning yourself to a few days of discomfort is far preferable to following the advice of certain authorities, who warn you off all uncooked foods and ice in drinks, condemning you, without any guarantee of safety, to a bland and unhealthy diet. Safety is also very much a state of mind. Exaggerated guidebook warnings can prevent readers from enjoying their trip by making them paranoid in areas where they are completely safe. Alternatively when their dire warnings are seen to be exaggerated, they may lull visitors into a fall sense of security in areas where they do have to be careful.

"The world is so constructed,
that if you wish to enjoy its pleasures,

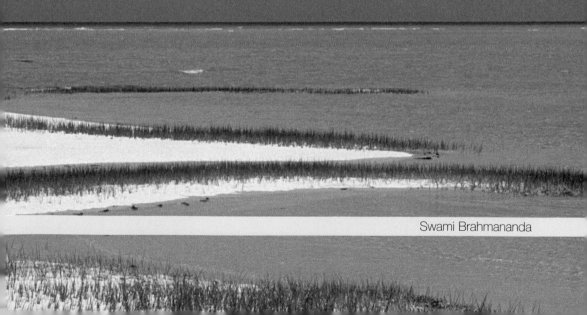

you also must endure its pains."

Swami Brahmananda

practicals: Valuables

Before leaving home, make two photocopies of your documents, leave one at home and pack the other set of copies in your luggage, making sure that it is separate from your real documents. Include: passport, airline ticket, travelers check receipts, insurance documents, credit cards, national and international driving licenses, and vaccination certificates.

Items such as watches, rings, earrings, and bracelets are safe to wear, unless it is your habit to remove them when you go swimming. In this case it is far better to leave them in your hotel safe or room.

Modern suitcases always have combination locks, but this is not always the case for pilot's cases and travel bags. Purchase padlocks for these if they have not been provided by the manufacturer. A small padlock will not discourage the determined thief, but it will prevent the opportunist from dipping into your luggage on its way from the plane to the carousel; or when it is left in the hotel lobby.

A daypack or backpack is not a safe place to carry your valuables, as they are too vulnerable to thieves who have developed ingenious means of getting at their contents. The safest option is a money belt worn under your clothes.

Practicals: Health

Common sense should be your guide with food. The ice, fresh fruit, and salads available at major international hotels and restaurants is likely to be safe, but exercise caution in inexpensive local restaurants and outdoor eateries. All drinks should come in sealed containers. When buying cookies and cakes, opt for anything in a sealed packet to anything on open display. Only buy fruit once you have checked that the skin is unbroken. Wash before peeling, and avoid letting the outside of the rind touch the pulp. If you cannot buy bottled water, you can use purifying tablets to make your own supply of safe drinking water.

A basic medical kit should contain the medications you routinely use, along with the following: anit-diarrhea tablets (loperimide), analgesic pain killer (aspirin, paracetemol, etc.), bandages, and antiseptic ointment. Carefully read the documentation provided with drugs that you buy over-the-counter.

Check with your medical adivsor and find out what vaccinations you will need before setting off on your trip. Common vaccines include: Diphteria, Hepatitis A, Hepatitis B, Japanese encephalitis, Meningitis A and C, Polio, Rabies, Tetanus, Tick-born elephantiasis, Typhoid, Yellow fever, and B.C.G. (tuberculosis).

chapter 8

right understanding: homecomings

meditation: "No matter what road I travel, I'm going home." Shinso

Among the Native American tribes of the southwestern United States, a traveler who returns after a long journey is treated as a stranger, even by his closest friends and kin, until he or she has become reacquainted with home. We, however, are brought up to believe in an immutable "I"—a fixed personality existing through time and space—and fall into the trap of believing that when we return to the geographical origin of our journey, we have returned unchanged to an unchanging place called "home." But the journey's end is only the beginning of another journey: the rediscovery of both home and ourselves, our perceptions of which have been subtly or dramatically transformed by our absence.

"When a traveller returneth home, let him not leave the countries where he hath travelled altogether behind."

Francis Bacon

returning

After years spent traveling and living overseas, I have come back to settle in London, perhaps to test for myself the truth of Dr. Johnson's much quoted assertion that "When a man is tired of London, he is tired of life; for there is in London all that life can afford."

I am sitting at one of the white plastic tables outside the Italian coffee bar in the public garden at Russell Square, at the very heart of London, in Bloomsbury, enjoying the chill rays of early April sunshine. It has just rained, and the asphalt paths are lustrous and clean. Russell Square is very far from being London's prettiest garden square, but it is one of my favorites, not only because the coffee is good, but also because it is in the center of London's intellectual "Bermuda Triangle," as it is within striking distance of both the British Library's new building and the British Museum.

Ahead of me looms the gray stone skyscraper of London University's Senate House—a building worthy of Stalinist Moscow or Fascist Milan for its monumental soberness. Behind me is the Russell Hotel, a handsome Victorian edifice, whose restaurant rejoices in the bizarre name of the Virginia Woolf Grill, Burger, and Pasta Bistro—an unlikely commemoration for the author of *Orlando* and *Mrs. Dalloway*. Virginia Woolf, the guiding spirit of the Bloomsbury group of artists and writers, famously lived in the area in the early part of the twentieth century, when it was still the center of London's publishing trade. She loved this part of the capital, describing it in 1924 as "…fierce and scornful and stony hearted, but as I say, so adorably lovely that I look out of my window all day long."

"We shall not cease from exploration
And the end of all our exploring
Will be to arrive where we started
And know the place for the first time." T.S. Eliot

sharing emotions

Even when I was studying or working abroad, I would return to London for visits. At first, I made a point of coming back to spend every Christmas here, but as the years passed, my visits became less frequent and shorter. After a two-year absence, several colleagues and I had been sent to a trade fair in Europe, and I was returning via London, where I was to spend a few days getting to know our British sales and distribution office.

I flew into London Heathrow business class, seeing it with the eyes of the businessman for the first time in many years, and getting some notion of what the English playwright Dennis Potter felt when he wrote of London's principal airport: "I did not fully understand the dread term 'terminal illness' until I say Heathrow." I decided to take a taxi into town—because I could claim it on expenses, and definitely not because it was more practical than the underground. I was rewarded with a forty-five minute traffic jam on the road coming into London.

I had a room on the upper floors of a hotel at Hyde Park Corner, which afforded me views of my native city I had never seen before. I looked down into the spacious grounds and inner courtyards of Buck House (as Buckingham Palace in known to the English). The palace had recently been opened to the public for a limited period every summer, and visitors can judge for themselves whether, as the Duke of Wellington asserted in 1828, "No sovereign in Europe, I may even add, perhaps no private gentleman, is so ill lodged as the king of this country."

The palace was originally a large country house built for the Duke of Buckingham in 1705. It was bought by the unfortunate George III in 1761, and completely redesigned by Beay Nash for George III's profligate Prince Regent, later George IV. The main façade in front of which tourists congregate every morning for the changing of the guard was added in 1913.

Looking beyond the palace, I could see clear across Green Park and Saint James Park, to the heart of British democracy and government, Whitehall, and the Houses of Parliament, and to England's "parish church," Westminster Abbey, built by Henry III in 1245, scene of the great ceremonials of state, as well as the crowded pantheon of the nation's literary heroes, whose memorials jostle for attention in Poet's Corner.

The vista on the Hyde Park side of the hotel took me back to the London of my childhood—beyond Knightsbridge and Harrods department store—to Kensington, with its elegant garden squares and their Victorian townhouses, the museum district, and Kensington Gardens itself, where I played under the statue of Peter Pan, sailed toy boats on the Round Pond, and swam in the Serpentine Lake. Many years later, I returned to Kensington Gardens to see for myself the thousands of floral tributes laid all around Kensington Palace after the death of Diana, Princess of Wales. In retrospect, it is difficult to convey what London was like when Diana's mortal remains were brought back from France and finally laid to rest.

As I watched Diana's funeral on television, I remembered that, in 1981, I had stood on a chair on the Strand, to cheer as she had driven back by coach from St. Paul's Cathedral where she had married Prince Charles. All of a sudden, I experienced a personal sense of loss that I had only felt before when my mother had passed away. Yet, I had never met the Princess, and I had shown little more than passing interest in the many column inches about her that daily seen to fill the pages of the world's press. I was not alone, as many others in England had been affected in the same way. The grief was real enough, but who was it really for, I asked myself. Was it for this unhappy young woman none of us really knew, or was it because her very public death had provided us with such vivid a reminder of our own mortality?

"And do not change.

Do not divert your love from visible things.

But go on loving what is good,

simple and ordinary;

animals and things and flowers,

and keep the balance true."

Rike

During a business trip to London (I lived in Japan at the time,) I was chauffeured to and from meetings by car or taxi and treated to meals in the kind of restaurants that only foreign businessmen with expense accounts go to dine. During an afternoon off I went shopping to buy presents for friends and co-workers. I was paying for the assorted fruit teas, shortbread biscuits, and wafer mints in Fortnum and Masons in Piccadilly, when I realized that I was looking forward to going "home"—that world of casual clothes, favorite bars and restaurants, and evenings out with friends. Only home had long ago ceased to be London, it was now in Tokyo on the other side of the globe.

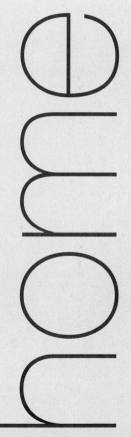

"We shape clay into a pot,

but it is the emptiness inside

that holds whatever we want."

Tao te Ching

travel on the mind

From being a citizen of the world, it seems, I have become a virtual prisoner of Bloomsbury, in London and I so rarely stray from its confines that occasional outings to visit friends in distant Kensington or Hampstead seem like major adventures. I feel no equivalent mental limitations, however, because around me I have "all that life can afford" in terms of intellectual pleasures, and my personal computer at home opens up the unlimited vistas of cyberspace.

"Inside yourself or outside,

you never have to change what you see,

only the way you see it."

Thaddeus Golas

histories

It begins to rain again. I could go home, which is now a few streets away, but I decide instead to take in the new exhibit at my near neighbor, the British Museum, perhaps the greatest repository of human memory. I cannot agree with the French poet and artist, Jean Cocteau (1889–1963), who likened museums to morgues—to me they are the very opposite, they are celebrations of humanity's cultural diversity and achievement. In the British Museum's galleries I can view the artifacts produced by cultures of which few other physical traces remain, or which are located in places inaccessible for reasons of geography or politics.

Instead of fighting through the tour groups and crowds at the main entrance on Great Russell Street, I make my way to the much quieter rear entrance of the museum, just across Russell Square in Montague Place. The museum owes its existence to the activities of one man, the physician and naturalist, Sir Hans Sloane, who spent his life and considerable fortune collecting, not objects made of precious stones and gems, but books, magazines, and paintings. Upon his death in 1753, he gave his collection to the nation, but it was not until 1847 that Sir Robert Smirke's imposing neo-Classical building was completed to house the collection which had expanded considerably over the intervening century. The final addition to the building, the spectacularly glass-roofed Great Court, which incorporates the old Reading Room of the British Library was opened in December 2000.

I make my way through the Egyptian, Assyrian, and Greco-Roman galleries, traversing, in a few dozen steps, three thousand years of human history, and make my way towards my favorite, and also the museum's most controversial exhibit, the Elgin Marbles that once adorned the Parthenon in Athens. Although it had been converted into a church in the fifth century and into a mosque in the fifteenth, The Parthenon, built by Phidias on the orders of Pericles in the fifth century B.C. to honor the city's patron goddess Athena, survived almost intact until the seventeenth century. Tragically, it was destroyed during the Venetian siege of Athens in 1687, when a Venetian cannonball set off the powder that had been stored in it by the Turks.

The sculptures that lay scattered among the ruins were bought by the Seventh Earl of Elgin (1766–1841), British envoy to the Sublime Porte, as the Ottoman empire was known, from the Turkish rulers of Greece, whose soldiers were using the Parthenon for target practice. Elgin sold them to the British Museum in 1816, and becoming the unwitting cause of a dispute between Greek and British governments a century and a half later.

Leaving the Museum through the imposing portico of main entrance, I go for a stroll through the neighborhood I now call "home." I am entering a district that perfectly suits anyone enamored of all things B.C.E.—Before Computer Era. Alongside the cafes, souvenir shops, and cashmere sweater outlets, you will find London's greatest concentration of antiquarian, specialist, and second-hand bookstores outside of Charing Cross Road, including a bookshop in Museum Street whose occult books and paraphernalia are guarded by a shrine to Sekhmet, the Egyptian lion-headed goddess.

In the galleries opposite, I browse through photographs, lithographs, and antique maps, but no visit to the area would be complete without looking in at the galleries whose windows are crammed with an amazing horde of natural and manmade treasures: ammonites fossils, multicolored natural crystal formation, Ming Dynasty figures, Roman glass bottles, and ancient Greek pottery.

I look longingly at an ancient Greek kylix for $300 and a Chinese Song-period celadon bowl for $400. I could easily fill up my apartment with these cut-price archeological treasures, but I always check myself. I have accumulated too many souvenirs already, and I do not need to own pieces of the ancient world to appreciate the beauty of its arts and the wisdom of its philosophies—as long, that is, as I have the British Museum on my doorstep.

The rain has stopped and the sun is out once more. We have seen the sun so little in this first spring of the new millennium that I am tempted to go back to Russell Square, where I buy what I promise myself will by my last capuccino of the day. I watch a Korean tour group marvel at the exoticism of a flowerbed full of red and yellow tulips, in front of which they photograph one another from every angle. It is strange to watch tourists experiencing the joy of being in a new city—as I have done so often myself—in the place that I call home.

"A monk asked Chao-chau 'If a poor

man comes, what should one give him?'

'He lacks nothing,' answered the master."

the traveler

I will never stop being a traveler.
My journeys are henceforth destined to lead
me along different paths on which I will need
neither passport, traveler's checks, nor
vaccination certificates. I will close with a verse
worthy of being the traveler's koan:

Without stirring abroad,
one can know the whole world;
without looking out of the window,
one can see the Way of Heaven.
The further one goes,
the less one knows.

"For my part, I travel not to go anywhere, but to go. I travel for travel's sake. The Great affair is to move."

Robert Louis Stevenson

practicals:

An Observation Exercise

When we travel, our senses are always alert, allowing us to discover the new sights, smells, and sounds of our surroundings. But when we go about our daily routine—commuting to work or school, or shopping we follow routes that have become so familiar that we walk or drive along them as if we were asleep.

The joys of discovery should not be limited to the few weeks that we are able to go on holiday every year. Next time you go out on a journey you are accustomed to making, make a point of looking for something new. It could be the detail of a building that you have never noticed, a tree or shrub that has come into bloom or leaf, or even an unusual sound or smell.

practicals: De-stressing

Zen only prescribes one form of meditation practice, zazen, in which you sit with your eyes open and your mind focused on your breath. Although this is the simplest form of meditation, it is also the hardest to maintain, because the mind is offered little to focus on to center and calm it. Other forms of meditation can be used in parallel with zazen to rest and prepare the mind. One such technique is creative visualization, in which the power of the imagination is used to center the mind.

To practise creative visualization, find a quiet room where you will not be disturbed. Sit or kneel in a meditation pose you find comfortable, or sit upright in

Meditation

a chair. Do not lie down as this will encourage drowsiness, and you may fall asleep instead of completing the exercise. Breathing deeply and slowly, inhaling through your nose and exhaling through your mouth, close your eyes, and imagine that you are walking through a natural landscape. The choice of the place you visit is entirely up to you. It could be a place you remember from childhood, or one that you have visited recently. Use your past experience of places that you have particularly enjoyed to create the most restful and pleasant place you can imagine. Once you have created your landscape, you are ready to move through it, imagining not just its appearance, but also its sounds and fragrances.

Sourcebooks, Inc.
P.O. Box 4410, Naperville, Illinois 60567-4410

TEL: (630) 961-3900
FAX: (630) 961-2168

Printed and bound in Italy by Amadeus
MQ 10 9 8 7 6 5 4 3 2 1

ISBN: 1-57071-616-1